After National Service, Tony Thorne read History with an exhibition at Jesus College, Cambridge. He then embarked on a thirty year career in the City and on Wall Street. One of his achievements was to be fired by Lehman Brothers. From 1978 until his retirement in 1990 he was Managing Director of Smith Barney in London, the US investment broker. He lives in Wimbledon. He and his wife, Carol, have two children and six grandchildren.

BRASSO, BLANCO AND BULL

TONY THORNE

Constable • London

Constable & Robinson Ltd
55-56 Russell Square
London WC1B 4HP
www.constablerobinson.com

First published in the UK by Rogerson Press 1998

Published by Robinson, an imprint of Constable &
Robinson Ltd, 2000, in association with Rogerson Press

This edition published by Constable, 2012

A copy of the British Library Cataloguing in
Publication data is available from the British Library

ISBN 978-1-78033-459-2

Printed and bound in the UK

1 3 5 7 9 10 8 6 4 2

ACKNOWLEDGEMENTS

The 'Brasso' and 'Blanco' trademarks of the 'Brasso' product are used with the kind permission of Reckitt Benckiser plc.

CONTENTS

INTRODUCTION

'Bring back National Service' is a not an unfamiliar cry these days, usually signed off by Lt-Colonel Grumpy from Tunbridge Wells. I doubt that the reintroduction of a mandatory and universal two-year military training for eighteen-year-olds that some elderly folk suggest would be the panacea for all our problems with today's youth. (Indeed I would be hesitant about introducing today's young men to the highly sophisticated weaponry that our armed forces currently deploy.)

However, one entire generation *did* serve for two years as peace-time conscripts. Two and a half million young men (no women!) did National Service and, for most of us, this provided a defining period in our lives that still has resonance after fifty or sixty years. Several quite important books have been written about National Service, and this is not one of them. But none of them has really attempted to investigate whether those that did National Service, and society in general, benefited from the experience.

When this book was first published in 2000, we celebrated with a party at the Imperial War Museum in London. Several of the characters who featured in the book dressed up as private soldiers in the uniform that we wore in the 1950s and paraded before a formidable Sergeant-Major from the Scots Guards. I recall the familiar clatter of army boots on stone steps as we descended to form up on parade. As we passed a couple of dear elderly ladies on the steps, I remember the startled look on their faces as they saw half a dozen sixty-something-year-olds flying down the steps in uniform. 'Don't worry,' said Tim Rogerson, who played a major part in the publication of this book, 'your country is in good hands'.

At the same time, the BBC was working on a six-part series for the radio about National Service, which was billed as an attempt to investigate the impact that National Service had on our generation. The presenter was Charles Wheeler, who had previously been the very distinguished Washington correspondent for the BBC, but who is probably best remembered today as the long-suffering father-in-law of our Lord Mayor, Boris Johnson. Not surprisingly, Charles Wheeler appeared at the book-launch party with a full complement of recording devices and interviewed as many of the attendees as he could. The atmosphere was nostalgic and jolly and, without exception, the interviewees shared wonderful humour with the microphone, ably assisted by their considerable distance from the events described and a fairly liberal supply of alcohol.

When the series was broadcast, none of our interviews was included. At first we were puzzled, but it soon became apparent why we had all ended up on the cutting-room floor; the BBC, or the producers or Charles Wheeler, had an agenda. It had already been decided that the conclusion would be that National Service consisted of two wasted years; two years of bullying, boredom and bestiality. In the programme that was broadcast, a series of actors, art critics and other celebrities bemoaned the dreadful time that they had spent doing National Service; luvvy after luvvy grieved about being ordered to clean the latrines with a toothbrush or paint the coals white.

I am not sure that this really represents the true experience of the majority. Many years have passed and there is no doubt that the notorious rose-coloured spectacles play a part in some of our memories of the time served, including those in this book. Additionally, it has frequently been remarked in relation to *Brasso, Blanco and Bull*, that 'it was all very well for you because you was a bleedin' h'officer', and therefore by definition it was an easier experience by comparison. I don't wish to get into this argument because hopefully it has no relevance to enjoyment of the following pages. I should point out, however, that it is widely accepted that the selection process and the intensive training at officer cadet school was considerably more demanding than the training carried out by the average conscript.

Anyway, the point I would like to make is that the picture painted of National Service as, at best, a wasteful experience and, at worst, a thoroughly corrupting influence, does not present the full story. National Servicemen had the opportunity to mix in a wider world than would otherwise have been the case. They could learn to drive a car or a tank, fly an aeroplane or sail a warship; they could learn German or Russian; they could play football or cricket or tennis or squash or run and jump or shoot, box, play hockey or rugby, play darts or 21 Aces. Whichever they chose, the facilities were the best they would probably ever experience in their lifetime. They travelled all over the world, from Hong Kong to Somalia, from BAOR in Germany to Kingston, Jamaica. Many fought and some died in Palestine, Malaya, Kenya and Korea. Most importantly of all, they were privileged to be absorbed and accepted by the existing army, navy and air force from whose rugged regular members they were able to learn a lot.

If National Service was so destructive of the moral fibre of that generation, it is hard to explain the reunions that carry on to this day where men, passionate and proud of their regiments, squadrons and ships, still gather all over the country to remember their experiences as National Servicemen.

The truth is that there is such a wide disparity in experience that it is impossible to form a judgement on whether National Service was a good or bad thing. It ended in 1961 and, after only a few years, the next generation had more or less forgotten there ever had been a call-up.

In 2000 I was doing a radio interview in connection with the original publication of *Brasso* when I was introduced as 'Toby Hall, who has written a very funny book about National Insurance.'

Tony Thorne,
London, August 2011

I

A MEDICAL EXAMINATION

It begins with a medical examination. It might have been July or it might have been August. It certainly was 1956 when I was summoned to attend a medical examination to check my suitability to serve my country for two years' national service.

Young men in uniform were commonplace in 1956. It was customary to see groups of soldiers, sailors and airmen in all public places. On or off duty, they were everywhere. It was rare to enter a pub or a cinema and not see several young boys, for that's all they were, in uniform. Most of them were only pretend servicemen, young men of eighteen or nineteen years of age undergoing the obligatory two years' national service.

Furthermore, the need for young men in uniform was recognised universally. The Second World War had ended only just over ten years before. Since that time the Great Powers of East and West had pointed their nuclear arsenals at each other in a continuous eyeball to eyeball confrontation. The Cold War was hotting up nicely in 1956. The fine balance between a dangerous peace and a lethal war would nearly topple again within a couple of months when Soviet tanks would roll over defenceless protesters in Hungary. Thousands were killed as Hungarians attacked the hated Soviet tanks with their bare hands.

East and West confronted each other around the world in a state of near-war. Hostilities on the ground had only just been suspended in Korea and, within months, my country would again be at war, this time in Egypt. Tension gripped the media. East and West ranged against each other arsenals of unimaginable destructiveness. There were itchy fingers on the trigger. Armageddon seemed likely. Defence of the realm was a deadly serious matter.

On both sides of the Iron Curtain the young men were conscripted. In the event of war my generation would be required to make the same sacrifice that the young men of previous generations had made.

This was the climate in which I was ordered by the War Office to attend a medical examination in Wandsworth. The army starts early and I had been ordered to attend at 7.30 a.m. The journey to Wandsworth from my home at Hampton took well over an hour and I had my first taste of the early rising that was to become a feature of my life for the next two years. I saw the world that morning at a time that I had been more accustomed to seeing at the end of my day rather than at the beginning. But it was unthinkable to be late and at 7.15 I had reached my destination. A primary school had been requisitioned by the Army and converted into a medical testing facility.

It was immediately apparent that I was not the only candidate for the examination. Several dozen young men were already waiting patiently outside the building. Men from all walks of life were quietly milling about on the pavement.

We were a motley collection of eighteen-year-olds thrown together by the chance occasion of an appointment for an Army medical. All of us were strangers to one another apart from one pair of identical twins and, even they did not speak to each other. By today's standards we would have made generally a fairly colourless crowd. Grey flannel predominated. Perhaps we might have claimed to be a little smarter, or at least, tidier, than today's youth, but we were nothing remarkable. It was virtually the same group that we see every time an old black and white film clip shows the crowd cheering Billy Wright's Wolves. Most wore a jacket and tie. The occasional jacket snaked its way down over the hips in the fashionable drape of the Teddy Boy, but most were just utility wear and most were grey. Trousers were narrow but they too were nearly all grey. Jeans were around but had not obtained the universality of today. Long hair had not yet been invented but that should not be taken to mean that we had no style. On the contrary, everyone had hair swept back from the temples, slicked along the sides and meeting at the back with a small projection from the back of the head known as a Duck's Arse. The only ones not sporting the hairstyle were sporting a hat instead. About a third of the company wore some kind of hat; not the sporty baseball cap favoured by all movers and shakers of today, but caps: cloth caps, felt caps, dirty old caps, even a few trilby hats. In order to demonstrate that one was at ease with the world it was required either to comb the Brylcreem through one's hair with a nonchalant flick movement of the comb or to clench a lighted Woodbine in the teeth Bogart-style. Most of our little gathering was doing one or the other and quite a few were able to do both at the same time.

At 7.30 a.m. precisely the main door was flung open by a very little lance corporal who displayed all the unease with which most military dignitaries confront civilians. He seemed unsure whether to bark out orders parade-ground style or just adopt the attitude of a cinema usherette. In the event, the decision was pre-empted as he was submerged as the crowd poured through the door.

Inside was a large school gymnasium. A few broken wall bars hung sadly from the walls; a dirty climbing rope hung from the ceiling; an old vaulting horse had not made it over its last fence and lay distressed in the far corner of the room. The only other furniture in this barren rectangle was a group of primary school benches. Because they had been designed for five- to eleven-year-olds, they were too small for full-grown potential soldiers. Those that sat on them looked ridiculous with their knees drawn up around their ears. Those that didn't sit on them felt ridiculous as they shuffled around the room selecting the correct pose. In those awkward few moments which precede any attempt at social intercourse the old props, the fag and the comb, were relied upon aggressively. At this stage there was not much conversation but much compensating body language.

The Royal Mounted Fag and Combs. If this was tomorrow's Army, then I was already quoting the Duke of Wellington.

Actually that is not true, I was not quoting anyone. In fact I was trying to be even more anonymous than everyone else. I was six months out of one of the smaller public schools and here were at least two hundred cockney lads, every one of them considerably bigger than me. I just knew that I was the only one in this company from a cosseted middle-class background and that, if I revealed myself, I would get my first experience of armed combat. My medical was shortly to reveal my height as five feet seven and a half inches and, even that was only scored after I had demanded a recount. The odds looked bleak and I knew that if I revealed my background by opening my middle class mouth my national service might begin and end on the same day. So as not to be cut down on the battlefield of the class war, I was not going to speak to anyone.

Others did speak. Gradually little groups formed. English reserve was broken down by the cheerful exchange of insults. Only in this country and in the Antipodes will a room full of complete strangers strike up acquaintance by hurling rudery at one another. Years later I spent much time in the United States and I still bear the scars from the mistaken assumption that this same social etiquette prevailed in that country. No way José.

After an hour of standing in the corner on my own, I eased my way inconspicuously on to a vacant space on one of the benches. The little group to my left were already conversing and I quickly saw which way the wind was blowing.

'Bleedin' lark this is. Reckon I'm OK 'cos I'm gonna throw one of me apoplectic fits soon as I get in there.' He gestured towards the adjoining room into which several men had already been summoned.

On this prompting the little group on the end of my bench produced a catalogue of ailments and disabilities which would certainly obtain disqualification from any Army. I was about to recoil in horror from these appallingly afflicted beings when it slowly dawned on me that most of the candidates for this particular exam had already determined to fail. For the first time the thought began to appeal to me. The more I considered it, the more the idea seemed to have some merit. After all there was no great disgrace involved in failure. I recalled that several of the country's leading sportsmen had been turned down for their national service. Colin Cowdrey had failed his medical because he had fallen arches. Just while I was contemplating my rather puny body to see where arches might have fallen off, he spoke to me.

He was sitting on my right, a great hulk of a man. He was about four feet tall sitting on a child's bench. A quick calculation suggested to me that he would be well over six feet tall if he stood up, which God forbid. He wore no jacket and the massive arm closest to me was covered in tattoos. A huge serpent was coiled around a naked lady and both rippled in tune with the enormous muscle in his forearm. Underneath was tattooed the single word in capital letters MUM and then, below that, a single sinister inscription BOURNEMOUTH.

He did not look at me as he spoke because we were pinned so close together on the little bench that, if he had turned his face towards me, we would have had quite a nasty collision in the nasal department. Instead he jabbed his tattoos into my stomach as an indication that his remark was addressed to me.

'Don't fockin' pee.'

All my short life flashed before me. It was obvious he was determined to pick a fight with me and was suggesting I had urinated on him as a 'Casus Belli'.

'I haven't. I didn't. Er, I mean, it wasn't me.' The dreaded sound of my own voice, the public school accent was amplified by a note of sheer terror. Heads along the bench turned; eyes stared.

'No, no mate. I said donna pee. Don't take a piss. 'Cos when you get in there,' he gestured towards the only door out of our room, 'they are gonna make you pee into a sodding bottle.'

'Oh,' I stammered, totally unable to understand where this conversation was leading. 'Very interesting.'

By now my new conversationalist had turned to face me. This had required some swivelling of his large frame such that everyone else sitting on our bench had been forced along domino fashion. This in turn drew even more attention to us.

''Cos if you can't do it they can fail you.'

This was becoming more and more confusing.

'But I, well, I thought that was the general idea,' I stammered.

He leaped to his feet. I was wrong. He was indeed well over six feet. Now the whole room was staring at us.

Not since Marcus Antonius at the Old Vic had I heard such an impassioned piece of oratory. Like much of Shakespeare this language was difficult and it was only after two months service in the Army that I was to become fluent in this lingo, but, even then, I could make out the general thrust.

Here standing before us was a man who was fairly pleased about his physical condition. He would be deeply ashamed to fail his Army medical and he saw it as his duty to serve Her Majesty. What is more, anyone who advocated any other course of action might as well square up to him right now and settle this whole matter with a little bout of fisticuffs.

It was pretty apparent that much of this diatribe had been addressed to me and by now the whole room was focusing on this corner.

'Er, well yes. I quite agree,' said my timid little voice. An ugly silence had descended on the whole room. In desperation I was just about to cast off all my reserve and burst into a chorus of 'Rule Britannia' when my new friend thumped me so hard on the back that I slipped off the bench and shot across the floor.

'So Don't Fockin' Pee,' he roared, pulling me back on to the bench and lowering his huge frame beside me. The silence persisted for what seemed like a century and then, slowly, a buzz of conversation resumed around the room.

My new friend turned to face me again.

'Spunky,' he said.

'Er, yes. I mean, thank you.'

'No, no. Spunky. That's me name mate. Spunky Reid. But most of me mates just call me Spunk,' he said, proffering his great hand.

'Oh, pleased to meet you,' I said.

'Well, what's your fockin' name?' He said.

'Tony, Tony Thorne,' I mumbled.

'Well, Tone Boy, don't fockin' pee.' This time he nearly broke three ribs as he jabbed me with his elbow.

An Army medical orderly was summoning us one at a time into the room beyond. About every ten minutes he would call a name in alphabetical order. This was going to be a long process. Reid and Thorne had rather a long wait ahead.

At around midday the orderly started handing out

half-crowns to those of us at the latter end of the alphabet and we were invited to go away and buy ourselves some lunch and be back in half an hour.

By this time Spunky Reid had attracted a small group of followers. I was no longer his only friend. About half a dozen had assembled under his leadership. These were the ones who, like myself, would not dream of faking an ailment to avoid serving Queen and country. We were the Patriots and my little heart swelled with pride at being one of them.

Two shillings and sixpence. That was a big shout in 1956 and, as soon as the half-crowns had hit the Patriots – or rather the Patriots M-Z – it was clear that the War Office had made a solid investment.

'Come on Tone boy,' said Reid. 'I know me way round 'ere.'

And we were off.

I absolutely revelled in Spunky's patronage. For some reason he had found me amusing and he made a point of advising the other Patriots that I was an OK bloke. ''E's a fockin' little toff. 'E's going to Cambridge after this war. 'Ow many of you lot's going to Cambridge?'

Spunky and the Patriots shot off down the street. This was his home patch and two quick turns down a side street and he led us to the 'Three Feathers'. It seemed a less than appropriate name for such a gallant gathering as the Patriots, but we all followed in Spunky's slipstream and burst in. The pub was quite crowded and there were several groups of young soldiers in uniform. Spunky made a point of diverting from his route to the bar to slap several of them on the back and yell 'Good on yer', in their ears as their beer slopped on the floor.

No one complained and we all jostled our way to the bar. On arrival our leader collected all the half-crowns. There had been seven of us, but one seemed to have done a runner between the medical centre and the pub. Spunky slammed six half-crowns down on the bar. 'Eighteen pints of mild,' he ordered. Then turning to the other Patriots, 'What about the rest of you?' He roared with laughter.

Three pints in half an hour. I was confident I could drink my corner, but I hadn't reckoned on mild. In fact I had hardly ever heard of mild. On my few visits to pubs I had always drunk bitter, but now I was confronted with the drinkers' drink of the 1950s. Strong and slightly sweet, it tasted awful. No wonder it disappeared from the scene in the 1960s, only to be replaced by the universal gnats' piss called lager.

We slammed it back. No problem. Times may change, but the effect of a little booze on young heads was the same in 1956 as it is today. I grew about six inches and appointed myself as second-in-command to the great leader. Suddenly we had formed into a group of great mates. The way to confirm our own fellowship was to be thoroughly obnoxious to everyone else around. Anyone who has stood at Stamford Bridge will be very familiar with the ritual. The group must choose a catchword or phrase and shout it in unison as frequently and loudly as possible. Our little special was 'Don't fockin' pee', followed by a quick chorus of 'Good old Spunky'.

We shot out of the 'Three Feathers' into the street yelling our anthem over and over again. Were we having a good time! We chanted our war cry all the way back to the medical centre.

There were still at least fifty sitting on the little benches waiting patiently when we burst in. Only three hours before I had been quite unable to open my mouth in this assembly, but now, after the miracle of three pints of mild, I was able to yell at the top of my voice, 'Don't fockin' pee'. Furthermore it was, without doubt, the wittiest, most sophisticated chorus I had ever heard.

By 3 p.m. the situation was getting a little tense. The chanting had died down and several Patriots were sitting cross-legged and grimacing as the Great Bladder Test moved into its final stage. Only Spunky Reid seemed quite unphased, chatting merrily with all and sundry. I sat on my little bench, white-knuckled, clenching and unclenching my fists.

We reached Q. The medical orderly popped his head around the door and called out 'Queer' and then corrected it to 'Queen'. This produced much ribaldry from all but the remaining Patriots, most of whom were now staring ashen-faced at the door. Spunky continued to chat away, seemingly quite unconcerned. At least R for Reid was going to come up before T for Thorne. I glanced desperately around the room, counting at least twenty remaining examinees and dreaded that 75 per cent of them were Smiths. This was going to be a very close call.

Just after 4 p.m. the orderly called my name. Groucho Marx, without the cigar, made his way towards the door. Bent almost double and with knees pinned together, like a girl in a tight skirt, I negotiated the door to confront my first military disaster.

To my absolute astonishment, the white-coated figure who greeted me on the other side of the door was a very attractive young lady. I heard something about a specimen as she gestured towards a small area of a long corridor cordoned off by a tatty old curtain. Behind the curtain was an old wooden stool. Standing on the stool was a little bottle about the size of a Marmite jar. There was nothing else, no other facility, no plumbing. Nothing.

Magnus Magnusson, many years later, played the role of the question-master on the popular television show Mastermind and, when he started to pose a question, but was interrupted by the buzzer, he used the catch-phrase, 'I've started, so I'll finish.' I could never watch him without unhappy memories of my Army medical sort of 'flooding' back.

Under the disdainful eye of the young lady in the white coat I was still doing my penance with a mop and a bucket when I was saved from further humiliation by a fortuitous diversion. Outside in the corridor a tremendous commotion was taking place. The non-Patriot who had threatened an apoplectic fit was on full throttle. His half-crown had been invested in a different liquid of the washing-up variety and he was foaming at the mouth like an over-fermented beer keg. He thrust his face into the floor and performed a series of thoroughly realistic contortions.

The young lady in the white coat had not really recovered from my little incident and this latest development was altogether too much for her. She was screaming hysterically for assistance.

A full sergeant of the Royal Army Medical Corps came at a gallop. He surveyed the scene, showing all the expertise of many years presiding over Army medical examinations.

I was still standing disconsolately in sodden trousers pathetically clutching my little mop. The epileptic fit was reaching a crescendo.

The sergeant made a quick assessment of the situation and decided to deal with the epileptic first. A mighty size twelve Army boot curved a perfect arc and he drop-kicked the dying swan to the other end of the corridor.

'Points for style bloomin' zero.'

'And as for you,' he turned to me, 'you can't piss your way out of the Army.'

2

CALLED TO THE COLOURS

I was called up less than a month later. Apparently my little accident at Wandsworth was not to be held against me and I was to report to Guildford railway station in two weeks' time between 10.30 and 11.30 a.m. I had even passed my medical in the top grade. This qualified me for service in the infantry and, if necessary, for active service. A railway voucher was enclosed to cover the cost of the journey to Guildford, one shilling and sixpence. At the bottom of my call-up notice was a paragraph in very small print which said that the Army could be quite dangerous, that the War Office would do its best to look after me, but could accept no responsibility if anything unfortunate happened to me. I had been selected to serve in the Queen's Regiment, the Royal West Surreys and I was to be Private Thorne 23339788.

On 27 September 1956 I alighted onto the platform at Guildford railway station at just after 10.30 a.m. I had attended the medical with a certain amount of trepidation, but it was as nothing compared to the actual call-up. This was the real McCoy. I approached this with king-sized trepidation. I really did not know what to expect, but the overwhelming anticipation was that I would walk into a wall of prejudice against the little ex-public schoolboy. For this latest test of my courage I had again dressed anonymously, no old school tie and cavalry twills for me. I wore an open-necked shirt and an old grey jacket.

Half way along the platform there was a little posse of the military. The reception committee consisted of a single private soldier wearing a sort of canvas waistcoat over his battledress. I was later to discover that he had achieved one of the most sought-after ranks in the British Army; he was a driver. There was also a young lance corporal whose function was to look junior and nondescript to set off the full majesty of the figure standing like a military colossus alongside. Three brilliant white stripes denoted a full sergeant. Standing stiff-backed and bushy-tailed, he held a small clipboard in one hand. His uniform was pressed from top to toe. Knife edge creases ran in all directions and his boots shone as no boots I had ever seen before. He wore the bright red sash of a duty NCO. On each shoulder he wore a blinding white shoulder flash of the Buffs. I had already been transferred to another regiment.

The first sergeant I ever met played completely against type. He called me 'Son' and checked my name off his clipboard. Then he welcomed me to the British Army and said I would be doing my initial training with the Buffs. This meant very little to me. He might as well have told me I was to join the Royal Canadian Mounted Police. Certainly I would have gone wherever he told me. At my school the word Buff was the common expression to describe the passing of wind, but I didn't think this was the time to mention it. Instead I listened intently to what this flawless figure of authority had to say.

In a voice that reminded me of one of my kindest uncles, he told me to go out of the station and look for an Army five-ton truck parked on the forecourt outside. I was to jump inside and wait.

As I walked, as smartly as I knew how, along the platform, I heard his pleasant voice from over my shoulder.

'Move yerself laddie, you're in the Army now.'

I scuttled along the platform.

How many ugly thugs would be waiting in the truck to attack me? Would they set upon me right away, or would they conspire amongst themselves during the journey and then beat me up when we arrived wherever we were going?

All seemed fairly innocuous in the station forecourt. There was a camouflaged Army truck sitting right outside. No one seemed to be around. I summoned up all my courage, took a deep breath, swung my little overnight bag over the ramp at the back of the truck and climbed in. There were only two occupants and neither of them looked overly threatening. They were both about the same age as me, eighteen. But, somewhat more surprisingly, both seemed to be about my size. In fact, one of them, who was sitting quietly in the far corner, looked even as though he might be smaller than me. Both looked totally downcast and not a word was exchanged as I sat at the near end of the truck close to the tailgate.

I nervously tried to view my truck-mates without incurring any eye contact. The little guy had what looked like a bag of tools sitting on the floor beside him. Our call-up summons had stipulated that we should bring nothing into this world. We were allowed a toothbrush and a razor, but that was about all, so I was mildly surprised to see the bag of tools.

He saw my eye settle on the bag and, in a somewhat apologetic tone, he said,

'Tools mate, I'm a plumber.'

I nodded understandingly. This particular little fellow seemed unlikely to attack me, but I was staying on my guard.

Nothing else was said and the three of us sat in a despondent silence. The minutes ticked by. Eventually the two at the far end of the truck exchanged a few pleasantries from which

I gathered that the plumber came from Brixton. The other one might have come from West Ham. It was hard to hear, especially as I had adopted the pose of a man totally at ease with himself. The conversation and this assumed confident pose were both interrupted by an enormous crash on the back of the truck, signalling the arrival of the next recruit.

The next arrival confirmed all my worst fears. Here was a thug if ever there was. Massive biceps flexed as he pulled his huge body over the ramp. His thighs were a little larger than my waist. He sat immediately opposite me and I observed his heavy jowls and dark, lively eyes. Don't pick a fight with this man. The words of a popular song of the time flashed through my terrified mind. Tennessee Ernie Ford was singing:

> 'Sixteen Tons. He weighed Sixteen Tons.
> If you see him coming better step aside.
> A lot of men didn't and a lot of men died—'

'Blimey,' he said, 'it's Tony Thorne.'

'Good Lord,' I said, 'it's John Webb.'

And there, in the back of a five ton Army truck, began a friendship that has continued until this day, over forty years later. The next few days and weeks would be full of the unexpected, but perhaps the most surprising development would be the number of young men that I would meet who would become friends and stay friends to this day.

John Webb had attended another school very similar to mine. The two schools competed with each other at every level and John Webb had been a sporting hero. All our lot knew John Webb. He had been a real thorn in our side on the rugby field and on the cricket pitch. He had been an outstanding full back in his school's record-breaking rugby team, as well as captaining the cricket team. He played cricket in the style of Ian Botham, twenty-five years before he was invented.

I had met John occasionally during our schooldays, but I could not claim to know him properly. Nevertheless, it was an enormous relief, as well as a total surprise, to see a familiar face.

'What on earth are you doing here?' I said.

'I'm in the Army,' grinned Webby, as he became known universally.

As we began to chat cheerfully together, the other two occupants of the truck seemed to shrink further away into the darkness at the far end. That we two should seem already to know each other was clearly incomprehensible to them. Webby waved to them with a fairly cheery 'Good morning', something which I had so far failed to do. This friendly gesture however seemed to increase their discomfort and we resumed our conversation in slightly subdued tones.

We quickly established two points of contact. First, we discovered that, if we survived the next two years, we were both going to Cambridge University. Not only were we both going to Cambridge, we were both going to the same college.

The great significance of our second discovery eluded us then.

My army number was 23339788 and Webby was 23339789.

However, within a very few days we would learn that all soldiers attach an almost mythical importance to their Army number. This is because numbers are issued in chronological order reflecting the date of enrolment and, since the whole system of the Army relates to seniority, the number is a telltale indicator of the length of one's time served. The lower the number, the longer one has been in the Army. It is quite incredible the enhanced status that attaches to a lower Army number. It might have been just comprehensible that a real soldier, that is a regular soldier, who might have been in the Service for several years, particularly if they included years 1939–45, would take some pride in the number of years he had served. But this same ritual was picked up by all soldiers, including national servicemen, whereby some strange superiority was achieved by how long one had been in the Army. Not so much in years or even months but often weeks, days or even hours could be seized upon to establish one man's seniority over another.

If we had really been soldiers, and not just civilian recruits sitting in an Army truck, I could have seized the initiative and taken command. The very least I could do would be to yell mindlessly 'Get some f . . . ing service in!' followed by a stream of terminal abuse. However, I was not at that precise moment feeling like taking command of anything. Neither Webby nor I had yet served even an hour and we were still pretty unfamiliar with the finer points of military etiquette, so we continued to chat quite politely.

Our conversation was eventually interrupted by the arrival of two more new soldiers. These two were already chatting to each other when they half jumped, half fell over the ramp of our truck. One was slim and fair-haired, with the face of a delinquent cherub. The other was very dark, tall and good-looking with a slightly sincere and questioning expression on his face. These were John Farrar and Tony Swinson. It was not surprising that they were talking to each other already because they happened to live next door to each other in Banstead in Surrey, though it had come as a complete surprise when they had met a few minutes previously on the platform.

John Farrar was a little older than Tony Swinson. Indeed, he was about three years older than all of us. He had been to yet another public school in our little circle, but had then embarked on a career as a surveyor. For this reason his call-up had been deferred which was the custom for people pursuing a qualification. Unfortunately for him, after three bouts with the surveying examiners, he had come off second best three times and eventually the recruiting officer had got him. At that time none of us knew how very fortunate this was for us. He was to become our father figure at the age of twenty-one and all the rest of us were to become totally in his debt for his helping hand during the times of unbelievable stress that lay just ahead.

Tony Swinson was the same age as the rest of our intake, but, unlike the rest of us, he was a gentle, quiet man who was a declared Christian. Little did we know the strength of character he would need to display shortly to cope with the blasphemy and the bullying which was known in the Army as Basic Training. However, right now, he was as pleasantly surprised as Webby and I had been to find a familiar face. What is more, as soon as he took his seat in the truck, he found he knew another face. He and Webby had played in the same schoolboy rugby team representing Surrey. He introduced Grandad, as the twenty-one-year-old John Farrar became known and Webby in turn introduced me. This was rapidly turning into an Old Girls' reunion. Four of us sat at one end of the truck while the two original inhabitants pulled further away into the anonymity of the far end. In deference to them, we continued to chat in fairly subdued tones. Even though we found ourselves thrown together with a small group from somewhat similar backgrounds, we all knew that this would not last. The Army just wasn't like this and we had better watch ourselves in case we got set apart as some sort of la-di-da clique.

To this day I have never understood how the call-up process worked. Why had this particular group been selected to report to Guildford on this particular day? In a rare glimmer of foresight the Army seemed to have called us up together so that our demob would coincide with the start of the academic year at the university. I don't recall if computers had been invented then and, even if they had, they would not have been able to work one. I can only assume that some bowler-hatted gent in the War Office had drawn up a list of recruits for this day, the majority of whom were starting at a university in two years' time. Whichever way it was achieved, five of the next six to climb aboard our truck would be attending university in two years' time.

One was Jumbo Fuller. Tall, fresh-faced and smart, he was the only one who already looked remotely like a soldier. Jumbo had been the senior prefect at quite a well known public school until one day he had brought the school cricket team back from an away match and had alighted from the school bus with a Senior Service cigarette still alight. He was greeted by the Headmaster. This bit of absent-mindedness had made Jumbo into a minor celebrity. This had been a hanging offence in those days and I even remember reading about it in a national newspaper.

Jumbo was charming and debonair. If Ian Fleming had been looking for a prototype for James Bond, he might have thought of Jumbo. Never detached from a cigarette, there was something instinctively correct about the way Jumbo dressed. Later, he alone would be able to present a picture of elegance even in some of the Army's most imaginative creations. He alone was to become a paragon of the parade ground and yet remain one of the most amusing and popular members of our little Army.

Another in this succession of arrivals on that day was called Simon Gillett. He could hardly climb into the truck he was so tall. At eighteen years of age Simon had already grown to six feet and four inches and he looked somehow as though the rest of his body was still trying to catch up. He had jet-black hair and heavy stubble on a rather white face. We were later to discover that Simon had a 5 o'clock shadow at breakfast time and a full beard by midday. As he stumbled over the ramp and fell amongst us, he looked like a cross between Dracula and Jack The Ripper. There was a sudden shiver of fright among the ranks at the sight of this latest arrival, who picked himself off the floor and placed himself awkwardly next to me. With all eyes now turned in his direction he pulled out a small book from inside his huge jacket. 'Madrigals of the Fifteenth Century'.

Simon Gillett was a man whose looks totally deceived. Scholar, poet and giant, here was a man who was later to share the same fate as me in the boxing ring. But, in the meanwhile, he struck up a conversation with another scholarly recruit about some rather obscure quotation from Homer.

We still maintained a fairly subdued tone to our conversation in deference to the other little group at the far end of the truck. This group had now expanded to three as it had been joined by a polite ginger-haired man who had said nothing but sat beside the plumber with a totally bewildered expression on his face. In fact it was not hard to discern the same expression on each of their faces. What had they done to deserve this awful fate? Was this some kind of conspiracy? Why had they been pitched into the back of a five-ton truck with a group of upper-class twits? Were they going to spend the next two years surrounded by a group of blokes talking about rugby and some Greek ponce? Heaven forbid.

Out of the corner of my eye I caught sight of the next arrival. There was no doubt to which group this one belonged. Dark brown suede shoes, or brothel creepers, were striding across the station forecourt towards the truck. A bold houndstooth jacket set off against cavalry twill trousers and a tie with all the discretion of the MCC. He was jauntily swinging a little overnight bag in one hand. Here was a toff if ever I had seen one. The little bag arrived first as he lobbed it nonchalantly over the ramp. It shot along the floor and came to rest at the far end of the truck. Then he vaulted athletically over the ramp, strode the length of the truck and sat himself down in the only remaining space, which happened to be exactly opposite the little plumber.

'Robin Berkeley. Tonbridge,' he said. 'Where were you?'

3

LEARNING THE LANGUAGE

Probably the Army had its own language at Agincourt. It certainly had its own language at Howe Barracks in Canterbury where our truck delivered us on 27 September 1956 and that same language was spoken in every British Army station around the world.

Most of us had naïvely expected to encounter some slightly different words or phrases. What we had not expected was the need to learn a totally new tongue. We had all been to the cinema and had experienced what we thought was 'Armyspeak'. We knew that all officers talked with a sort of chipper, upper class cheerfulness as they shrugged off mortal danger. We had plenty of experience of jaunty Richard Todd or little Kenneth More, with or without legs, chatting away in initials.

'CO at GHQ. Tell your NCO chappie we all US. OK Roger and out.'

We were pretty familiar with the heroic cockney corporal spitting out one-liners as his limbs were amputated one at a time without anaesthetic by a medical orderly on the battlefield.

Surely there was nothing in the Army vocabulary that we had not heard a thousand times before.

The first word that requires our attention begins with f. It is quite inconceivable that any book, film or programme can represent any aspect of life in the British Army without an almost continuous flow of this one word. Not only is this the most important word in the Army's private language, it is quite frequently the only word. It is certainly the Army's only adjective and, even on those rare occasions when a soldier can find another adjective, like, for instance, 'shitty', it must always be qualified with the preferred 'f' word to become 'fockin' shitty'.

Unfortunately, the 'f' word is not only an adjective. It is also a noun, a pronoun and an exclamation mark. It is even most people's name, as in Sgt Fock, or Fred Fock. Whereas civilians might punctuate their conversation with 'Er' or 'Um', soldiers use just one word. Furthermore, it is the mainstay of the Army's language at every level. Soldiers, or ORs (Other Ranks), pronounce the word to rhyme with 'Dock', whilst officers pronounce the word to rhyme with 'Duck'.

Very few soldiers who have served in the Army for more than a month can put together a sentence without using the 'f' word at least once. Most words that consist of more than two syllables will have to be hyphenated to inject the 'f' word, as in 'See you to-fockin'-morrow', or 'Sergeant-fockin'-Major'. Soldiers greet one another 'Mornin' Fock', or 'Whatcha Fock'. No one in the Army ever needs to remember anyone else's name because this one all-encompassing word covers everybody and everything. Furthermore, there is nothing pejorative in calling someone 'Fock'. On the contrary it is regarded as a very friendly form of greeting as in 'Hello mate'.

The word has no dictionary meaning. It has just become standard Armyspeak, a reactionary word used on every occasion. I now know how totally misleading all those post-war films were. In the real Army, battleground burials would have sounded the last post and some corporal would have recited 'dust to fockin' dust, ashes to fockin' ashes'.

Some soldiers, particularly the experienced sergeants, of whom we would meet many, could actually combine the 'f' word with other so-called swear words to give some truly colourful expression, but most soldiers capitulated to a sort of monosyllabic dirge consisting of very little other than the single word. So conditioned did soldiers become to the constant repetition of the 'f' word that, when an event of real consequence occurred, they were frequently lost for words. I recall seeing the regimental carpenter put a nail straight through his finger and bring the whole carpentry shop to a shocked silence when he yelled out 'bother'.

Since a large number of the participants in this story made conversation with such ingenuity that they only required this single word, conveying the message through a variety of subtle shifts of emphasis, it would be quite limiting to try to remove it from the text. However, bearing in mind that, even today, this word still retains that peculiar property of shocking some people, I have attempted to translate wherever possible.

There are some other words in this language which might require some explanation.

The Army's second favourite word is 'grip'. This word, like that other, is constantly repeated over and over. It generally relates to all forms of discipline. The most usual form is 'get a grip', which means just about everything in the Army, but is probably best translated as 'pull yourself together'.

One can 'get a grip', 'get a grip of oneself', 'grip' someone or 'be gripped'. One could 'get a grip' of some inanimate object like a rifle or one's boots. One could 'get a grip' of one's hair which simply meant that the last remaining stubble on top of one's head was shaved off. Any person in any form of authority would either shout or mutter 'get a grip' at all times and in every situation. At a later stage in my military career I recall being greeted to a new unit by the commanding officer, a full colonel. He delivered a half-hour lecture describing in great detail all that lay ahead and emphasising the long tradition of fighting morale, which we had inherited. At the end of a delightful and civilised speech he concluded with the traditional 'Carry on, Sergeant Major' (pronounced 'Saaarnt Mayjaw').

The saaarnt mayjaw took charge, 'Right, you all heard what the officer said. Get a fockin' grip.'

'Getting a grip' did however have a more sinister meaning, especially when related to basic training. In this context 'getting a grip' is better translated as bullying or terrorising. It implies the use of all psychological or physical means to intimidate. When our truck arrived at the regimental headquarters of the Third of Foot, the Buffs, the diminutive lance corporal who started shouting at us informed us that he was under orders to 'grip' us. We were about to find out that very specific meaning of the word.

We have to familiarise ourselves with other parts of the Army's native language.

'Idle', pronounced 'idol' is the Army's general word of disapproval or criticism. It is very rarely used without the prefix 'fockin'', so the word that one in fact has to observe is really 'fockinidol'. When used by an officer it becomes 'fuckinggidle' with considerable emphasis on the 'gg'. This is another all-purpose Army word. Of course, most soldiers are called 'fockinidol' most of the time. But this word too can be attached to almost anyone and anything. One can have an idol rifle or an idol pouch. The most common charge laid against any soldier is that he is idol on parade. I was once told that Adolf Hitler had an idol war.

'Jankers' is another word we all needed to know about, because this was one of the most common forms of punishment. 'Jankers' required the offender to parade at some specified time in full battledress. This consisted of all the usual encumbrances which made it virtually impossible for any soldier to move on the battlefield, compounded by a tin hat and a rifle with a bayonet plus a huge pack on one's back. For most of us it was a real achievement to be able to maintain a standing position in all this gear. If one was on 'jankers' one had to run a specified number of times around the parade ground, usually accompanied by a cheerful NCO from the physical training section dressed in running gear to set the pace.

A few other words and their meanings that might not be all that familiar could include the following:

(Students should of course remember that these words or expressions may not generally be used without the 'f' word as prefix.)

Gungy	Dirty
Mank	Dirty
'Orrible Little Man	Me

4

VERY BASIC

Our Army truck was not the only one collecting a new intake of recruits that day. Several other trucks had picked up various additional groups from different venues around the south eastern part of England. In all, about fifty reluctant debutants had joined the same regiment on that same day and they had all converged on Howe Barracks on a hill just outside the cathedral city of Canterbury.

This was the regimental headquarters of the East Kent Regiment, the Buffs. For my part, I had never previously strayed into East Kent in my life, but the ancient tradition of serving one's own shire did not apply to national servicemen.

Howe Barracks was a modern military establishment. There was a pale yellow hue to the uniform brickwork of the buildings that was not altogether unattractive in spite of the pronounced institutional character of the architecture.

The overwhelming feature of the camp was a commitment to security. Heavy iron gates slammed shut behind us and the entire compound was surrounded by a high and intimidating wall. It was apparent that we were unlikely to be leaving for a while. Only later did we come to appreciate that the wall served another purpose as well: it made it impossible for anyone from outside to observe the indignities inflicted on us in the name of basic training.

Trucks were arriving from all directions. They each came to a halt on the parade ground. As each one halted it was attacked by a small group of screaming uniformed maniacs who hurled themselves at the ramp of the truck in a furious and totally unexpected assault.

'Get out! Move yer fockinselves. Get yer 'orrible arses out of there!'

The contents of our truck flung themselves out of the truck all over the parade ground. Quite terrified by this sudden change of address, we jumped, fell or hobbled out of the truck and started to run in all directions pursued by these shrieking tormentors. None of us had ever been subjected to such a verbal assault before. Nor did we realise that for the next sixteen weeks this would become routine. We were about to be 'gripped'.

Quite suddenly we found that we had lined ourselves up in a single file. The screaming assassins, in a well rehearsed move, had backed off and in their place, and standing directly in front of us, was L/Cpl Prudence. We were to be 'gripped' for the next sixteen weeks and the man in whose grip we were to be placed was standing here.

He was no taller than I was and he sported the most pathetic excuse for a moustache on his curled upper lip that I had ever seen. Some people can assert themselves by their presence or even by their manner, but Prudence had rank, as well as a moustache. There, gleaming on his arm was a white chevron or stripe denoting he was a corporal. At this particular point in our careers that little stripe conferred an authority upon him which was greater than anything we had ever experienced in our lives. He may have been small, but this was our Mr Big. Our truckload had now turned into No. 1 Squad of 3 Platoon and Cpl Prudence was introducing himself to us. He was very much in charge.

When I re-evaluate Cpl Prudence from a distance of over forty years, I have to concede that he was probably quite normal. He had trained as a boy soldier and was now a full-time career professional. He was probably no older than us. But, at the time, he seemed like a creature from another planet. The fact was that he had been programmed to terrify us and all the time he was himself terrified that he might not be terrifying us enough. He was haunted by fear; the fear that some NCO senior to him might think he was deficient in the 'beastly' department. His little moustache was intended to disguise him as an adult, but nothing could disguise the nervous disposition, which was to make Cpl Prudence's exercise of absolute authority extremely dangerous. I don't know whether he knew already that nearly two thirds of his squad came from a background slightly different from his own, but, in any case, it was only a matter of time – minutes not hours – before he found out. This would add mightily to his insecurity and cause him to attempt to 'grip' us with an almost hysterical intensity. It is no surprise to me to learn that Cpl Prudence pursued a very successful career in the Army. Long after he presided over our ill-assorted crowd, he continued to get a grip and he eventually reached the top of his trade as a top-ranking Warrant Officer.

The Army had an infallible formula for moulding recruits. It consisted of continuous harassment and virtually no sleep. It is hard to believe that a group of semi-educated adults could be intimidated by a pint-sized illiterate with a dopey moustache, but we were like putty in his hands. He was a lance corporal and we were sheep to the slaughter.

But even before we could play our part as sheep we needed to be kitted out. With Prudence snapping at our heels, we hurtled at the double to the quartermaster's stores where we again formed up in single file. Petrified soldiers. We had already discovered the terror of being singled out for individual abuse by the corporal.

'Oi. You – Bumface!' The dreaded finger of Prudence pointing at me. Pray God he is pointing at the bloke next to me. 'Come 'ere!'

With bated breath we waited outside the quartermaster's stores where we were fitted out one at a time. Each of us collected a surprising amount of clobber. I was astonished to find there was even a tailor inside the store. To date I had little experience of the cosy world of Savile Row and it was somewhat incongruous that my first introduction to the mysteries of chalk and pin should be in these circumstances. Each recruit was fitted out with two suits of battledress, or BD. The tailor ran the tape over my trembling body and barked out my innermost measurements, while a soldier kneeling beside me noted it down on a clipboard. 'Bow legs'. 'Right shoulder drop'. The Buffs' regimental tailor knew his onions. Even though he had to work in a material that resembled asbestos, the finished product was an exquisite suit.

The name battledress is completely misleading. Any idea that we would soon be actually wearing our new soldier suits, even our second best suit, was a total myth. We would iron them, fold them, caress them, but it would be a long time before we actually wore either of them. Then we would only wear them on ceremonial occasions. No soldier in his right mind would dare wear his prized BD out in the field. If the balloon went up and we had to go to war in our best BD, we would all be mincing about like a group of tarts trying not to spoil the arrow-shaped creases in our tunics.

What we were actually going to wear every day for the next ten weeks was an altogether different suit called denims, which were also issued to us at this time. These were stacked in a huge pile in the corner of the quartermaster's store. As each recruit finished with the regimental tailor, one of the staff hurled a set of these shapeless garments at him. Unlike the painstaking attention to the BD, these were issued more or less in the order they had been stacked and with no particular reference to the shape of the customer. You took what you got. If we like to think that our new BD gave an impression of soldiery, denims gave the impression of the chain gang. No clothing I have ever worn has been more successful at draining away any trace of human dignity, yet we would be expected to spend many unhappy hours trying to iron some shape into these most shapeless of garments.

We collected some other little nasties as well, like two brand new pairs of boots. In the next few weeks these boots would assume almost religious properties. We were in the infantry and an infantryman's boots take over his life. When issued, these boots are not shiny but dull. The surface is covered by hundreds of tiny little pimples looking like black tapiocas. These have to be smoothed away by a technique involving a candle, the back of a metal spoon and melted boot polish. In the next few weeks I would come to despise these little black pimples even more than Cpl Prudence. Every single one has to be individually bulled away. We were each issued with one new pale yellow duster, which played a vital part in this painstaking exercise. This same single little duster was also needed to work on the shine on all the little metal bits we acquired – belt brasses, gaiter buckles and cap badges. For these we were issued with one only tiny can of some foul-smelling liquid called Brasso. This paragon of all cleaning fluids became the British Army's secret weapon in 1905 and, to this day, is the only accepted medicine for cleaning brasses. It tastes awful.

In a matter of minutes the little cloth was grimed in a cocktail of melted boot polish, Brasso and dried spittle. And yet success could only be achieved in these delicate tasks if one had a piece of the cloth that was still virgin. Soldiers are likely to kill for a tiny clean corner of a duster.

Our boots, like our BDs, were graded. No. 1 boots and No. 2 boots. Our No. 1 boots became more precious to us than life itself. They were only actually worn on ceremonial occasions which meant that they never really got broken in sufficiently to be comfortable, but that didn't really matter since they spent so much more time in our hands than on our feet. Even though rarely worn, No. 1 boots were the focal point of every kit inspection. They would sit, hopefully glistening, on the end of the bed craving a word of encouragement. Our whole world rotated around our No. 1 boots. Our military careers depended on them. Before our basic training was over we would be on first name terms with every member of the squad's No. 1 boots. They would become like newly born babies in a maternity ward; the focus of all attention. Each pair had its own personality following hour after hour of spit and polish, sometimes all through the night. Tiny circular movements with a dirty little duster interrupted only with the splash of fresh spit and the huff of hot breath finally produced that peculiar high gloss shine like patent leather. All around the barrack room there were triumphs and disasters and we each knew every minute detail of everyone else's boots.

We all got berets. They were black shapeless things when issued. But the beret also quickly established its own particular personality. It too had to be broken in. When newly issued, the Army beret is fluffy and pansy. It perches on top of the head with its weight equally on either side. It announces 'new recruit' as clearly as the army number. When properly broken in, the beret denotes 'manhood' more than any other single piece of equipment. The shiny headband shoots horizontally across the forehead exactly one and a half inches above the eye. The main body of the beret is moulded to the shape of the soldier's head. It is no surprise to anyone who has ever worn a beret in anger that the heroism of whole regiments is described by reference to this little garment. When Paras are referred to as 'Red Berets' there is legendary symbolism in the name. It takes on average about fifteen hours of steaming, ironing and cursing to get the shape of a beret right. Then, at last, with a little bit of luck, the little black bugger will begin to look manly, sloping gently rightwards away from a gleaming cap badge. No one can perform heroics with a thing on their head that looks like a cowpat.

We were issued khaki belts and gaiters. These have to be Blanco'd. Blanco is not white as the name might imply, but khaki. It is like a slab of chalk, which must be dissolved with water to exactly the right consistency, so that it can be painted on to the webbing smoothly. In fact it produces tiny lumps like mother's gravy, which then increase in size when they dry on the webbing. The belt has little brass clips and the gaiters have little brass buckles at the opposite end to the black leather straps. The brasses must be shone with Brasso and the leather straps must be polished with boot polish. One of the miracles of military design is that all these cleaning materials are chemically allergic to one another. If the tiniest spot of Brasso makes any form of contact with the Blanco on the webbing, a small white ring appears which remorselessly spreads outwards in ever-increasing circles until it forms a huge unsightly stain. No man has ever discovered any method of removing this stain other than re-painting the dreaded Blanco about two hundred times. Even then, one can collapse exhausted into one's pit thinking that the damned spot is out, only to be greeted by it poking its head out anew at 5.30 a.m. just half an hour before the morning inspection.

Steel helmets (or helmets steel, because the Army has a curious sort of back-to-front language), mess tins and housewives were issued. A housewife is pronounced 'hussif' and is a little white cloth folded into a tiny handbag shape in which are nestled a needle, some cotton (khaki) and a thimble. Forget about machine guns and mortars, these are a soldier's real friends because he has to spend the next few hours sewing little name-tags on all his new kit.

We had vests and pants, long woollen. No music-hall comic is complete without them. But the real *'pièce de résistance'* must be the famous jungle greens. These were long green cellular drawers. Presumably these were issued in case we were called upon to fight in the tropics. The Army deserves credit for its far-sightedness in covering this eventuality, but unfortunately this was about all the famous jungle greens did cover. They were designed with an open fly. It really did not make much difference whether, as the tailors would say, one dressed to the right or to the left, the famous fly stayed open.

Philby, Burgess and Maclean gave away some pretty strong stuff to the enemy, but it all would have paled into insignificance compared to the secrets that our national servicemen revealed. Always attack in the warmer parts where our lads would be sporting their jungle greens. Not one of our fine infantrymen would be able to move more than half a dozen paces without stopping to adjust his dress.

New recruits were running hither and thither spilling socks, grey, woollen or shoes, black, PT for the use of, as they scrambled to get their kit back to the barrack room. In actual fact shoes, black, PT for the use of, was another military joke because, when issued, these were not black but brown. Only after many hours messing around with black shoe polish could these little devils be called black. Then each time we paraded for PT the black boot polish got all over our hands and the vindictive PT instructors started every session with a hand and shoe inspection.

Then, finally, we paraded outside the Armoury to draw out our rifles. We were each issued with a blunderbuss.

They were called Lee Enfield rifles and they were the very same that old Tommy had taken off to each of the last two wars. They were heavy, cumbersome weapons that frequently shot round corners. Each rifle was accompanied with a gleaming bayonet about eight inches long to be stuck on the end of the rifle for use in hand-to-hand combat. I later discovered that it took me about five minutes to attach my bayonet to the end of my gun. If the Zulus ever got over the barricade, my chances would be slim, but, nevertheless, it was comforting to see the flash of steel, even if this was one more item to clean.

We had to guard our rifles with our lives. To mislay a rifle is the most heinous crime a soldier can commit. The penalty is court martial. In war the penalty could be execution by firing squad if anyone could find one of the wretched things to shoot straight. The inside of the barrel of the rifle had a curious twisted indent that was supposed to ensure the correct trajectory. However, since most of these weapons were more than thirty years old, this also served as a repository for little pieces of dust and grease. The rifle barrel had to be cleaned with a thing called a 'pull-through', which was a fairly accurate description of what it was supposed to do, together with a little strip of material called a 'four by two'. This rifle cleaning was a miserable, painstaking operation. Since we were likely to be thrust into action at any time of day or night, both we and our trusty friend had to be in a permanent state of readiness. To ensure that this was the case there were snap rifle inspections at all times of day and night. The rifle barrel had to have a twenty-four hour shine. The penalty for the tiniest speck of dirt up the barrel was too terrifying to contemplate. I still shudder at the memory of the awful cry, 'gungy rifle'. No wonder the British soldier would go to almost any lengths to avoid firing the bloody thing.

For the time being most of these horrors lay in the future. All we knew on day one was that all this clobber, including the rifle, must be stowed away in the metal wardrobes that stood next to our iron beds.

It was a somewhat shaken group that re-assembled in our barrack room. Following the shouted instructions of our great leader Cpl Prudence, we changed into our denims. Mine would have fitted Webby and vice versa but swapping was not allowed. Then we had to perform our first military task. This was not to launch some fearless attack on the enemy, but to sew little labels showing our Army number on to every item of kit. Furthermore, the sewing had to obtain the approval of the corporal item by item. Anything less than a perfect stitch job and it all had to be done again.

Day one and we were about to experience the crippling routine that was to be our lot for the next ten weeks. Cpl Prudence would set the tasks relating to some or other piece of equipment. Then he would show us his own and we were required to get ours up to the same standard. Always there would be an inspection at six the following morning and we would all sit on our beds in total silence for hour after hour while we tried to achieve the required effect.

This sombre scene lasted way into the night. The pressure was unbearable as each recruit huddled over a boot, or a belt, or a cap badge, praying that it would suddenly undergo a transformation. On this first long night no one spoke apart from Cpl Prudence. He prowled around the room emitting the occasional scream of disapproval. If the scream was addressed to any particular individual, then that soldier was required to leap to attention, such that the boot he was working on would fall with a thud on to the concrete floor taking off any shine that said soldier had been able to apply.

We were fearful, but the man who was most fearful was Prudence. Next door to our room were two other rooms identical to ours. They each housed a similar squad of new recruits, namely No. 2 and No. 3 squad of our platoon. They also had their equivalent of Cpl Prudence and, when we all paraded together as No. 3 Platoon at 6 a.m. every morning, it was life and death that our squad did credit to our little leader. The arbiter would be Cpl Jones and the difference between Cpl Jones and Cpl Prudence was four inches and a full stripe. In other words Jones was a full corporal compared to Prudence who was only a lance corporal. How we dreaded meeting someone twice as powerful as Prudence.

Night and day fused together. We toiled away through

the small hours. One or two of the brave lads collapsed with fatigue to be roused by a prod from Prudence. All we could think of was the dreadful deadline of six o'clock. Finally, even the supreme command fell silent.

Suddenly there was a disturbance from the far end of the room. I saw Jumbo Fuller pick up a piece of old newspaper that he had been using to protect his blanket while he worked on his boot. He leapt to attention and, in his best BBC accent, read out the headline, 'I say, chaps. Listen to this,' he announced. 'Shower of shit in Shropshire. Man killed by flying turd.'

5

MEETING A MOLE

Our squad, No. 1 Squad, was all in the same barrack room under the watchful eye of Cpl Prudence. There were eighteen in all, excluding the Führer, who also had a bed in the same room. All the original truckload that had travelled down from Guildford were in No. 1 Squad and we were joined by the larger part of another truckload which had come in from Edgware. Of the total eighteen we were divided about equally between ex-public school types, 'the la di fockin' da lot' as the Corp called us, and another group of equally nondescript recruits.

There were no fewer than three Irishmen. Their only interest in serving in the British army was subversion and they did not show much interest in that. They kept their own company to the exclusion of all else and indulged in conspiratorial conversation. Their principal method of subversion was to disobey every instruction. It was never very clear to the rest of us how much of this was a deliberate plot and how much of it was the exercise of a natural talent. But, either way, it served the purpose of deflecting some of Cpl Prudence's anger away from other incompetents in the squad, of whom there were several.

The little plumber was still with us. It turned out that his name was Reg Plummer, which seemed appropriate. He also turned out to be a cracking good little soldier and a cracking good little colleague as well. Within a few days his kit was almost as well bulled as Prudence's. He just had that natural skill with his hands that made light work of spit and polish. His pack and his pouches stood in their correct position atop his metal wardrobe, squared off, erect and creamily Blanco'd. His blankets were always folded into a perfect square. But much more important, he was full of help and advice to all around him. He showed the giant Simon Gillett how to iron the pimples off his enormous boots. He tried and failed to mould the devout Tony Swinson's beret into the shape of his head. Poor Swinners was one of God's people, but his beret simply declined to answer his prayers. As Reg Plummer entreated, 'It's no good all that praying. It's just turning your beret into a fockin' halo.'

And it was a fact. However much Swinners, and indeed all of us, including Cpl Prudence, tried, his beret just refused to take shape. Even after ten weeks Swinners was still parading with a thing like a frisbee on his head.

The rest of the squad included some other very cheerful cockneys, full of humour and life, and some very dull and sullen figures, who made it pretty clear that they resented the Army and everything and every one associated with it.

Down my end of the room I was fortunate; first and fore-most because Cpl Pru was down the other end. But also, and I would come to appreciate this even more, because I had two great mates, one on either side.

Webby found the whole kit thing quite easy. Within a few days his boots began to acquire that peculiar gleam we all sought and he began to turn into something beginning to look like a soldier. He was also able to find the time to laugh at my efforts. In a pattern that repeated itself all around the room, Webby got his kit up to scratch and then turned to help me. He spent almost as much time on my boots as he did on his own. As a joint effort my kit slowly began to pass muster. I could never aspire to the best in the squad, but, after many hours of unremitting toil, I just began to take shape.

On the other side was John Farrar, old Grandad himself. He had been a big star in his school cadet force and he rapidly emerged as one of the real luminaries of No. 1 Squad. In addition he had that maturity which comes with twenty-one years. He also turned into a latter-day saint. As we all sweated and panicked over our wretched boots and kit, John would tour the barrack room often well into the night. Like Henry V on the night before Agincourt, John Farrar mingled with the troops and administered to the sick and faint of heart. With a spit here and a polish there, old Grandad would make his rounds, encouraging everyone, always finding a word of praise for even the most disastrous efforts.

There was a terrible ordeal three times a day. This was called 'mess', which is a well-chosen Army word for meals. In our case it was not necessarily all that appropriate because the food at Howe barracks was not at all bad. But meals were nevertheless a terrible ordeal.

This was because of the inspection that took place before each meal rather than the meal itself.

A shout of 'Mess' from the corridor outside our barrack room was the signal for us to grab our knife, fork and spoon, together with our white china drinking mug and race outside. There the ordeal began. We were required to line up in single file holding our white china mugs at the high port. This inspection was a Biggy. All three squads would be lined up in the corridor and this inspection would call for at least two, and sometimes even three, corporals. When we were all assembled, the pantomime began.

Cpl Jones pulls up opposite me. He peers into my spotless white china mug.

''Ere look at this, Cpl Prudence.'

Cpl Prudence scurries alongside Cpl Jones.

'What's this in there?' shrieks Prudence, pointing his little index finger inside my mug.

'Er, it's the bottom of my mug.'

'CORPORAL! Call me CORPORAL. You shithead. What's that in your fockin' mug? You . . .'

'Er nothing, CORPORAL.'

Prudence to Jones, leering. 'What's that in that mug, Corporal?'

'Sheeet!' screams Jones. ''E's got shit in his mug.'

Prudence to me, 'Now what's in that fockin' mug soldier?'

'Shit, CORPORAL.'

'Louder,' scream Prudence and Jones in unison. 'Louder.'

'SHIT, CORPORAL,' I scream.

'Blimey,' says Prudence to Jones, ''E's got shit in his mug.'

Jones peers into my mug much as Sir Lancelot would have peered into the Holy Grail. 'What are we going to do about it Corporal?' He asks earnestly of his colleague.

'Smash it. Smash it,' they cry out gleefully together. Then they fight each other to grab the mug from my hand and hurl it down onto the concrete floor where it smashes into a thousand pieces.

New mugs had to be purchased from the quartermaster's store and the stock market saw the price of North Staffordshire Potteries Ltd move to new heights daily.

This ritual was repeated three times a day, every day and the corporals never tired of it. Often the corridor looked like a snowstorm. Twice I brought a brand new mug and had it smashed the same day. On one occasion the whole of No. 3 Squad had their mugs smashed. Mug-smashing was a perk of Corporaldom and they loved it.

In the next sixteen weeks our humanity was stripped down to its bare essentials. It was impossible to retain any semblance of dignity in these barrack rooms. Nothing could be hidden from anyone. Every facet of one's innermost character was exposed for all to see. There was no escape, no airs, no graces, no polish or personality could escape this fearful penetration.

And the most remarkable bonding began. The greater the humiliations heaped upon us, the more our little squad clung together. No other system can achieve so readily the creation of a group of people, be they a squad, or a platoon, or a whole regiment, who so quickly become dependent upon each other. The Army moves in a mysterious way, but, if the purpose of training is to create units that identify together and subdue the individual to a common cause, then there is some real intellect lurking behind every page of the Army training manual.

The skills required to survive basic training were pretty unevenly distributed amongst our squad. Some, like Jumbo, John Farrar or Reg Plummer, seemed more or less born to it. They soon acquired a real pride in their achievements, while the rest of us were filled with admiration.

'Cor. Get that Farrar. He's only lost his goat's head.'

The regimental cap badge featured a Tudor dragon carrying a standard with a cross on it. Every one always referred to it as a goat. When the cap badge was newly issued this little creature was quite finely fashioned in brass. But from that day onwards it was the set intention of every soldier to Brasso the little goat into oblivion.

A real soldier, i.e. one who had got some service in and was no longer a recruit, would swagger around with a thing stuck on his head that looked like a gleaming blob.

Everyone knew every detail of everyone's kit. Like Farrar's cap badge, Jumbo's left boot was a masterpiece, but poor old Swinners' beret remained a disaster. Soldiers were constantly moving around the room lining up in silent admiration in front of some piece of kit, then scurrying back with tears of emotion in their eyes to renew the battle with their own item. After a few days we began to get to know our fellow victims in the other two squads that formed part of our platoon.

Our horizons gradually expanded as we got acquainted with two more squads of boots and belts and kit. We were soon moving not just within our own room, but as far afield as No. 3 Squad, which was two rooms away. News of success or failure with any item spread quickly and soldiers would rush into another room to congratulate or to commiserate. We soon became nearly as familiar with the other two squads as we were with our own. We knew who had stuffed a sock inside his beret, or who had used cardboard in his pouches.

Scattered throughout the three barrack rooms were about fifty young men from every background. They came in all shapes and sizes. The only thing we all had in common was that we were all about the same age, we were all conscripts and were all in No. 3 Platoon. There was a chap called Evans in No. 3 Squad who had played regularly for Crystal Palace Reserves and had even had a couple of games for the first team. Another in the same squad claimed to have had a sexual relationship with a female. This was an even more unusual distinction amongst eighteen-year-olds in 1956 and everyone crowded around to hear the details.

But perhaps the most celebrated of the whole group was another ex-public school type in No. 2 Squad. He was called Anthony Hole and his reputation, as one of the outstanding schoolboy sportsmen of his generation, had run ahead of him. He had attended the same school as Ted Dexter and had even outshone him with his sporting achievements. Not only had he been head boy, but also he had captained the school team at every major sport: rugby, cricket, hockey and athletics. This was almost unprecedented. Furthermore, his prowess as a rugby player had already singled him out for special attention in the Army. There was one certain way to escape the routine of the Army and that was to excel at sports. Anyone who reached a high standard at football or rugby, anyone who could run or jump and especially anyone who could box, was assured of a few short cuts.

Forget Brasso and bullshit, think tracksuit and train. In the British Army, squad competes against squad and regiment competes against regiment. The Army competes against the Navy and Air Force, and the Combined Services compete against the World – or they did in those days. The horizons of an Army sportsman knew no bounds.

Anthony Hole, or the Mole as he became known, was already a hot property. He was required to play rugby for the Army and this marked him out for special treatment. No one shouted at him and threw his mug half way down the corridor. He had special diets prepared and lovely Army nurses caressed his hamstrings. His name was mentioned only in hushed tones in our barrack room. I had never met the Mole, but I was well aware of his reputation.

One day I was queuing in the ablutions at 5.30 in the morning. It was necessary to stand in line to wait for access to one of the limited number of basins. As I shivered in my pyjamas, I found myself standing alongside a man with curly hair and a distinct smell of embrocation. For some reason he was wearing his jungle greens, but I knew I was alongside the great Mole.

'Hello,' he said in a diffident, slightly despairing voice. 'Isn't this absolute hell? I hate it.'

Here was a man without any of the bravado I had expected of the great athlete. I had finally met the Mole and here began another of the lifelong friendships that began in the Army.

As the line moved slowly forward, I made the acquaintance of the platoon's outstanding sportsman – Renaissance Man queuing pathetically outside the ablutions, all exposed in his jungle greens.

6

THE MAN WITH A CROOKED FOOT

What John Farrar was to spit and polish, Jumbo Fuller was to the parade ground.

Marching is an art. One might think that walking along in step with others, swinging one's arms, is a fairly undemanding exercise. Nothing could be further from the truth. Marching properly is like playing golf. Some have a natural eye and the coordination to make it look like child's play. Others simply cannot do it. Furthermore, those that cannot do it can very quickly infect those that can. To march along putting forward the right arm and the right leg at the same time to be followed by the left arm and the left leg is enormously difficult. But put fifty men on a parade ground under the glare of a parade sergeant and about half that number will achieve it with ease.

However, Jumbo was a model marcher. Stiff-backed, beret clinging to the side of his head, the slightest hint of a swagger; Jumbo Fuller was an object lesson to us all.

Whenever an example was set before the whole platoon, it was always Jumbo. Quite simply, he just looked the part.

One member of our platoon was called Martin Baldwin.

He was six feet tall, fine looking, normal in every sense. But he just could not march without putting his right leg and his right arm forward at the same time. Later, he was the only one of our whole platoon to make a bank manager happy. He became a financial whiz. He set up several computer companies and bought and sold them so successfully that he became a multi-millionaire. He told me that, for him, making money turned out to be as easy as falling off a log. During his national service days, if you hád put him on a log and asked him to fall off, he would have stuck to it like glue. Every time we were on the parade ground poor Baldwin would be hauled out of the line and forced to practise marching all on his own. Up and down he would march until he got it right. But the moment he was restored to the ranks all hell would break loose. Poor Baldwin would immediately revert to form and, within seconds, the whole file behind him would slip into a sort of backhanded goose step before crashing to the ground in a heap.

'No-3-Platoon, By the-Left-Queeek-March-Baldwin-Get-Out-Of-There-You-Fockin'-Great-Idiot.'

If marching is an art then saluting is high drama. It really deserves a chapter to itself. A soldier's salute is a dead giveaway, a bit like the first service of a tennis player. You can see in a trice whether he is going to be any good. Watch a guardsman salute and you will see the seemingly effortless action to which every soldier aspires. The whole body remains motionless, perpendicular. Everything moves at right angles. The arm moves like a disembodied limb. In one graceful move, the arm sweeps up in a full arc until the right forefinger strikes a point exactly one inch above the right eye. The palm of the hand is full-face outwards. The position is held for a count of 'Two, Three'. Then the hand races down by the shortest route to snap the soldier back to attention. The real stars, and these are the fellows who troop the colour, allow themselves one tiny indulgence. As the hand snaps into position against the forehead, they permit an almost imperceptible quiver, as when an arrow strikes its target. But this is advanced stuff, certainly not to be attempted by new recruits.

This is the text book salute. There are others. The most common recruit salute looks like a bent hairpin. Recruits are consumed by anxiety and in their eagerness to complete the movement smartly they tend to produce a travesty of a salute. As the arm hurtles upwards most recruits have an irresistible desire to bend the head down and sideways to meet it half way. Usually head and hand meet at about 3 o'clock. Sometimes they don't meet at all or, sometimes they collide with a sickening thump.

Officers, on the other hand, do not really salute at all. They make a gracious gesture of acknowledgement, for they think it is they who are being saluted. This in fact is not the case and most experienced soldiers and NCOs have a special expertise in making this clear to the officer. The salute is in fact directed to Her Majesty and the officer is only the recipient because he holds the Queen's commission. Nevertheless, most officers spend many secret hours in front of the mirror to develop their very own saluting style. It's a sort of 'You're welcome', as the Americans might say.

But it still can be a very grand production, especially from an officer called an adjutant. It is he who usually accepts the salute on the parade ground and his reply should be a very artistic affair. Most good adjutants appear on horseback and the salute has to be compatible with this rather challenging position. Anything too violent might frighten the horse. This could be dangerous on a large parade ground so the adjutant works on a salute that combines a certain arrogance with military precision, usually a close call between a sort of flyaway wave and a Heil Hitler. In our next few months of service we were to have first hand experience of some of the most notorious adjutant salutes in the British Army.

*   *   *

Meanwhile, back on the hill outside Canterbury, No. 3 Platoon was gradually taking shape. By now we had met Sgt Parker. He only appeared on very important occasions and it was clear to us, because of the enormous fear he engendered in Pru and the other corporals, that this was a man who required the greatest possible respect. He looked the part: tall, fair-haired and with a bristling blond moustache. He had an enormous barrel chest that looked as if it had been designed to hang medals on. In fact he didn't have any medals because he was just too young to serve in the war and thereby pick up the array of gongware that went with active service. But this in no way deterred him from thrusting this great upper body forward as if he expected HM to pin a whopper on him at any moment. Furthermore, he would have been an outstanding candidate because what he did for the Army, he did extremely well.

Mostly, he was the king of the parade ground and he was a fine drill sergeant. Orders came rumbling up from that great chest basso profundo, slowly, deliberately at first, then rising a couple of octaves until the final order was shrieked out like a high-pitched banshee. We didn't always move in the right direction but it was impossible not to move a mite sharpish when Sgt Parker's orders hit the airwaves.

He was immaculate in his appearance. Boots like pools of light, battledress creased and pressed like a suit of armour. He turned the human body into a series of straight lines. His belt and beret strap were in a perfect horizontal line and the creases down his legs and arms were in a perfectly vertical line, a sort of marching Pythagoras. And he scared the living daylights out of No. 3 Platoon.

After several weeks under Sgt Parker's expert tuition we gradually began to form a unit on the parade ground. It was not yet exactly one perfect wedge moving as one man, but, if we dropped out Baldwin and one or two others, we did begin to display some semblance of precision.

I never rowed, but one of my friends who was President of Oxford University Rowing Club, becomes ecstatic when he describes the exhilaration of pulling in a first class eight when the combined effort sings the boat through the water. A platoon drilling in perfect synch is the same. It takes many hours of gruelling practice but, when it all comes together, it raises the spirit to be a part of it.

One day Sgt Parker broke the news to us. In just under three weeks time No. 3 Platoon would take its place on the adjutant's parade. This meant that we would form up with the whole training battalion, some eight platoons in all, under the command of the regimental sergeant major.

The adjutant himself would take the salute and we would parade around to the stirring music of the regimental band. I can still recall the tremor of excitement as Sgt Parker announced that we would be wearing our best BD. Oh! Delirium! Now I know what the Tiller Girls felt like when they were chosen for a Royal Command Performance.

Anyone with experience of amateur dramatics will appreciate the build-up in tension that became the hallmark of our barrack room over the next three weeks. The Army thrives on competition. Already we had experienced heavy doses of our squad beating Cpl Jones' squad, but now it was a case of our platoon looking better, marching better, and shining better than the other platoons in the training battalion. We practised day and night. Sgt Parker screamed and sobbed at us. One minute he would be thundering death threats at us, the next minute he would make huge emotional appeals to us, just like some theatrical Luvvie during rehearsals.

As the great day approached Cpl Prudence became a man possessed. He rushed his little self around the barrack room trying to bring everyone's kit up to a perfect pitch for the occasion. His nervousness infected us all. Everyone was helping everyone else with his kit. The whole barrack room spat on my boots until the magic cocktails seemed to do the trick and they suddenly burst forth into a great black shine. But we still had the problem of Swinners' beret. It simply defied us all. Pru shrieked at it, steamed it, cajoled it, ironed it and swore at it. Nothing would mould it into the shape of old Swinners' skull. Maybe it would be easier to reshape Swinners' head, and serious consideration was given to this possibility. Then, one night, after hours of toil, Pru suddenly lost it. He grabbed the offending beret off Swinners' head and threw it across the room. Then he tore across the room and leapt on it like it was a poor dead cat and kicked it all around the place. Seven weeks work was undone at a stroke as the beret hurtled through dust and dirt and skidded across the floor. Finally Pru picked it up and hurled it at Swinners while the whole barrack room stood in a stunned silence. Pru had run amok.

There was only one thing for it. Swinners had to join Martin Baldwin on sick parade on the day of the adjutant's parade. This was a terrible waste because the rest of Swinners was pretty smart. His boots were well up to scratch and his gaiters were in the top league. Furthermore he was one of the taller guys in the platoon and he looked OK in action, but there was nothing that could be done. No. 3 Platoon would have to parade without Swinners. The die was cast.

The whole platoon had to reorganise to adjust to Swinners' absence. It mucked up the lines because he had occupied a fairly prominent place in the front row. Now the whole chorus line had to be re-jigged. The enormous Simon Gillett was the right marker. This was unavoidable because he was considerably taller that anyone else. But it was far from perfect casting. Simon was a little ungainly as he tended to stoop somewhat, his five o'clock shadow made him look a bit like a gypsy. Even if we shaved him immediately before going on parade, he still had a beard by the time we took the final salute. The right marker is the fulcrum of the whole platoon and the only way Sgt Parker could lessen the impact of the great bear was to surround him with his best players. Jumbo was right up there alongside Simon, and Swinners used to come next. Now this all had to be rearranged. Robin Berkeley, who had developed into a fine looking soldier, got the nod and moved up alongside Jumbo, even though he wasn't really the natural selection on height considerations. All this re-organisation had to be undertaken when we had less than a week before the dress rehearsal so this added greatly to the pressure on all of us, especially Sgt Parker. But nobody cracked.

Day after day we practised. The whole parade ground was covered with platoons practising different drills. Platoons were marching and wheeling in all directions. There was a big premium on navigation; even trained drill sergeants are capable of making an error. If two platoons inadvertently marched into one another, we had been trained not to flinch. Never break ranks; always stay in step; never anticipate the word of command. We would simply march on straight through the ranks of the oncoming platoon with heads held high. Any soldier who found the resulting shambles the slightest bit funny was shot. In addition it was recommended strongly that you always supported your own sergeant in the post mortem on the traffic accident. Amazingly, many a punch-up in the NAAFI was attributed to the fierce loyalty of members of a platoon defending their sergeant against some other clown who couldn't even read the Highway Code.

As platoons always parade with their tallest men on the left and the shortest on the right, when we turned to our right to break into a perfectly coordinated march, the taller men were at the front and the smaller men at the rear. One of the difficulties in this formation was that it was necessary to ensure that the tall guys up front didn't take their normal stride. If they did, the little fellows at the back would find themselves having to march like Groucho Marx. It was always difficult to convince the tall ones to abbreviate their stride because they were inclined to feel acutely self-conscious mincing along with little steps. Simon Gillett, as right marker, had to set the pace for our platoon. He was always quite good in the beginning at curtailing his giant stride, but, as we got under way and as the preening coordination of it all began to seize him, he would tend to forget this requirement and start to stride out like King Kong. I was the back marker so I was always marching along with enormous strides and swinging my arms like a windmill.

The day of the adjutant's parade finally came. Many of us were unable to sleep the night before; the anticipation overwhelmed us. Would it be a bright day? Would that last minute Blanco of the belt be dry? What if I dropped my rifle?

In the event it was a brilliant sunny October day. The whole of the barracks sprang to life at 5.30 a.m. For two hours every barrack room rang to the sound of feverish preparation.

'Are my trouser creases in my best BD straight? How do I look Webby? Can I borrow that last clean patch on your duster to give my boots their last buff? Oh Ducky, is my lipstick on straight?'

And suddenly we were all out on the parade ground. Way out ahead in the distance was the tiny figure of the adjutant. It was a tiny figure partly because he was some fifty yards away and partly because he was a tiny figure. His name was Captain Minto and his nickname was not important. I had come across him once before. One evening I had been walking back to the barrack room from the NAAFI when he approached, mounted on a huge charger. A group of soldiers just ahead of me had jumped to attention and bent sideways in a classic recruit salute. This had frightened the horse, which had bolted. Poor Minto had a frightful fall from grace. By the time I had gathered myself together to snap up my salute Minto was sprawling and his mount was hurtling past me in the final furlong.

'Never mind salutin'. Stop the horse you f . . . in' cretin.'

These were the first words I heard from a commissioned

officer since I had joined the British Army. I marvelled at the priceless diction in adversity. It brought to mind Olivier and Richard III.

Now here he was again. He had parked his horse but had replaced it with a huge and cumbersome sword, which hung precariously at his side. Because Minto was small of stature and the regimental sword looked something like Excalibur, his movement was severely restricted, but somehow he managed to retain some dignity as he joined the parade with a sort of hopping motion.

The regimental sergeant major sensed his approach and wheeled towards him in a blur of red flashes and huge wooden pace stick. The massive figure crashed to attention within inches of the tiny adjutant, not unlike the Flying Scotsman hitting the buffers. The peaked cap never moved as the smartest salute in the whole battalion soared headwards. The salute cracked like a whip within one inch of the adjutant. Minto didn't flinch. Instead he let go with his own notorious little acknowledgement. A little flutter, a sort of randy little wave and the adjutant started to wail into the cool October morning.

'Carry orn Saarnt Mayjaw.'

One massive swivel and a crashing of the brilliant boots into the parade ground and the RSM was facing the entire parade.

'Thee First Battalion Thee Royal Regiment of Thee Buffs. By Thee Left Quieeeek Mar!'

The drum beats. Four hundred left feet shoot forward as one.

And we were off. Around the parade ground we marched. We swaggered. The band played. The sun shone.

Each platoon sergeant marched alongside his platoon, with his head held high. Staring straight ahead, Sgt Parker could still detect the slightest imperfection. A stream of instructions flew sideways from a mouth that didn't move.

'Look up, look up, Gillett you great fockin' giraffe,' murmured the ventriloquist.

'Chest out Thorne. You little prick.'

Just when everything seemed to be going well and as the band launched into the Dam Busters March, disaster struck.

'Saarnt Mayjaw,' cried little Minto from the distance, 'There is a man theagh in No. 3 Platoon with a crooked foot. Have that man seen to.'

No. 3 Platoon! My platoon! Panic struck. Oh my God, whose foot has fallen off? Could it be mine? I dared not look downwards.

Suddenly the giant RSM was striding alongside our platoon. He pointed out the offender with the crooked foot to Sgt Parker and Parker yelled out.

'Gottim, sir, I've got 'im, sir. Private Fuller, sir. Man with a crooked foot, sir. I'll have 'im seen to, sir.'

In one great move he yanked Jumbo out of the ranks and doubled him across the parade ground while the rest of us marched on forlornly.

7

THE KING OF DENMARK

Three weeks later we were selected. One minute we were in our familiar barrack room in Howe Barracks, the next minute we were in a totally different barracks at the bottom of the hill. Like most things in the Army it all happened so quickly we didn't really know what was happening. Certainly no one solicited any opinion from us.

There were two quite separate barracks in Canterbury. Howe Barracks were the regimental depot and headquarters of the Buffs. At the bottom of the hill stood Wemyss Barracks. These barracks were a special training headquarters for all PL's from the Home Counties Brigade. The initials PL stood for Potential Leader. The Home Counties Brigade consisted of those infantry regiments, which were manned by soldiers who came from London and the immediate surrounding counties. It did not include the Guards who did everything exclusively because they were exclusive, and it did not include the Royal Marines who were a sort of hybrid, half-infantry and half-seamen, and marched funny. But it did include East Surreys, West Surreys (or the Queen's as they were called), Royal Fusiliers, Royal West Kents, East

Kents (The Buffs), Hampshire, Royal Sussex and Middlesex Regiments. Even a few misnamed representatives of the Intelligence Corps crept in.

Out of the latest band of recruits in each of these regiments someone had applied some selection process and chosen those of us now stationed at Wemyss Barracks. The basis of selection could not have been too arduous because most of No. 3 platoon at Howe Barracks re-appeared in No. 95 Squad at Wemyss Barracks. Jumbo brought his crooked foot down the hill. Thank Supreme Headquarters, Webby and John Farrar were here. The giant philosopher Simon Gillett had grown another full beard on the ten-minute truck ride down the hill. Word had it that the Mole was to join us later after he had played a rugby match representing the Buffs. Swinners was here with his godforsaken beret. Robin Berkeley was here too, exuding bonhomie. Even Baldwin was here!

Wemyss Barracks had been built two hundred years earlier and had been regularly condemned as unsuitable for human consumption. The so-called living accommodation was a series of wooden huts that had been built to house the horses before the Crimean War. There was no form of heating anywhere and, by now, we had moved into a vicious, freezing winter and yet we were all elated to be there. We had survived the first hurdle in the selection process, which could lead to obtaining the Queen's Commission, a peaked cap and a swagger stick. Everyone at Wemyss Barracks now hoped to be selected to go forward to take the series of tests, which were called the War Office Selection Board, WOSB, or Wozby. So everything now depended on being selected to go forward to Wozby and we were to start the process of looking keen and enthusiastic at all times and in all conditions. We were led to believe that Big Brother was watching us day and night in order to detect any signs of un-leaderlike qualities.

Wemyss Barracks made Howe Barracks look like the Savoy. Here the ablutions were a tidy sprint from our room and the

water in the taps was not even tepid. The cookhouse was a
ramshackle shed where not all the rats belonged to the Royal
Army Catering Corps. The gymnasium looked like some
weird torture chamber with mysterious instruments hanging from the walls. The parade ground was pitted and scarred
with the footmarks and shufflings of generations of march-
ers and stampers. Yet, whether we were lining up in the open,
outside the walled ablutions at 5.30 a.m., or racing across to the
gymnasium wearing our little red T-shirts and black sneakers,
we had to exude enthusiasm for all things military if we were
to meet our destiny at Wozby. Much as we hated this dreadful place the one fate we dreaded even more was being sent
away from it. To be returned to our unit, or RTU'd, was the
great punishment dangling over us. This meant that we had
been found unsuitable for further consideration as a Potential
Leader and, therefore, unable to present ourselves before the
Selection Board. This would mean that we would be ignomin-
iously returned, whence we had just come, to rejoin our unit
with failure written all over our best BD.

We did not really know who was watching us. Nor did we
really know what the elusive leadership qualities were which
we were supposed to display. Clearly intellect was not among
them. It seemed more likely to be a physical, bulldog sort of
thing. At five foot seven inches it did not come naturally to
me to present the right kind of body language so I determined
to compensate with a calculated, and wholly artificial, cheerfulness in the face of all adversity. I slept with a false grin on
my face in case some passing spy should think I was lacking
keenness. This newly acquired enthusiasm, and my height,
was later to contribute mightily to me being selected for the
inter-squad boxing match.

Wozby was on everyone's mind all of the time. If one passed,
then it was off to the challenging world as an officer cadet. I
had visions of uniforms dripping with gold braid and talking
all Ya-Ya. If one failed, it was back to the old unit again. But

there was a third category. This was called 'Deferred Watch'. This meant that the candidate had displayed some officerly qualities, but not enough to pass. In these cases the soldier was sent back to the PL camp and 'watched' to see if the missing half of the leadership qualities might develop. These were the fellows who made up the junior NCO command at Wemyss Barracks. They were appointed acting lance corporals and had to pass the test by taking command of the various new squads of PLs. They were on a hiding to nothing.

Our acting lance corporal was called Cpl Heath. He was one of those pleasant chaps who was basically much too nice to succeed in this environment. To make matters worse for him, he had been at the same school as the Mole and some others in our squad. This made his mission even more impossible. He was trying to impress his superiors and, at the same time, trying to appeal to some generosity of spirit, which he mistakenly thought might reside in the squad. He was a slightly ungainly figure who had a rather ponderous appearance on the parade ground. He was renamed 'Sloth' Heath and I think he enjoyed the next few weeks even less than we did. Whereas Cpl Prudence had barked out commands like a machine gun, punctuated with the required military obscenities, we now had Cpl Sloth,

'Now look here, chaps, we really must move along. Do try. I mean, well really. Oh, Baldwin. I say.'

We were the junior squad, No. 95 Squad. There was a total of five squads, each consisting of about fifty hopefuls. Every two weeks the senior squad graduated and most of them went off to meet their fate with Wozby. A few of them trickled back to tell the tale. These were the ones who were 'Deferred Watch'. But all the rest disappeared. The successful Wozbiers went off to cadet school. The unsuccessful ones returned to their units to serve out the rest of their national service. As one squad left, so another one arrived. The squad at the head of the parade when we arrived was No. 91 Squad and, when they disappeared, No. 96 Squad lined up behind us and we moved forward a few paces.

While the acting lance corporals were nearly all national servicemen who had themselves just been through this training, all the rest of the NCOs were real soldiers. The Army uses its best NCOs to train its leaders and Wemyss Barracks was staffed with the best that the Home Counties infantry battalions could muster. Sgt Hastings was in charge of No. 95 Squad. He was not as fearsome a figure as Sgt Parker had been up at Howe Barracks. He was an older soldier. He might even have been aged over thirty. To us he was a veritable Sgt Methuselah, who went about his duties with a somewhat world-weary expression. His many years of service had included unspecified activities in the recent little troubles with Adolf and this had entitled him to wear a great deal of medal ribbon on his BD. His service had also included fairly sustained contact with a bottle, which caused him to slur his commands slightly. On the parade ground he was fond of telling us that we could judge the failure of every movement simply by listening to it. A successful unit does, of course, move as one man and, in every parade ground movement, the whole squad makes just one sound, with every movement made together. As the squad halted, or sloped arms, or came to attention there should be one collective sound. In our case this was not always so and we got used to the despairing cry of 'Lishen to it. Lishen to it', to the extent that this particular cry became the catchword for No. 95 Squad, most of whose members spent their off-duty hours repeating the sarge's favourite expression over and over.

But the Big Star at Wemyss Barracks was Sgt Major 'Bomber' Wells. He was the outstanding company sergeant major in the Home Counties Brigade. As a young sergeant he had led his men up the Normandy beaches through a hail of bullets. From the moment he had dragged himself out of the sea he had marched up the beach as though he was still on his beloved parade ground, while his men ducked and weaved behind him. He was decorated twice before the war was over and had then made a real career for himself in the peacetime Army. He had the regulation sergeant-major-issue moustache and every inch of him proclaimed his profession. He it was who was really in charge of the PL training battalion. He presided at the daily morning parade and he controlled every aspect of life at Wemyss Barracks. Furthermore, because he was a consummate soldier, he was liked by all. He even had a sense of humour that he demonstrated frequently for the benefit of the whole assembly on parade.

We had reverted to much the same sort of regime that we had endured up at Howe Barracks. Apart from the freezing cold and the appalling condition of the barracks themselves, the only real difference we could detect was the heavy sarcasm that seemed to be directed at us continuously. Every training sergeant had his own way of referring to the fact that we had been singled out as Potential Leaders.

'Baldwin, how many fockin' O levels have you got?'

'Eleven, Sergeant.'

'Christ, eleven! Was marching one of 'em?'

'No, Sergeant.'

After two weeks Sgt Hastings shared with us a major piece of news. Apparently our worthiness to present ourselves before Wozby would be determined not solely by him, but also by our platoon commander and company commander. These were gentlemen who so far had made no obvious appearance and yet they were apparently assessing us. This immediately confirmed our worst fears that these officers had been hiding all the time in the ablutions, clasping a clipboard, while we had all been singing our little chorus of 'Lishen to it. Lishen to it.'

Now, apparently, one of them was about to break cover because, according to old 'Lishen to it' himself, our platoon commander, who was called 2nd Lt Bellamy, was going to inspect us the next day. There was a sharp intake of breath as though from one man as this little bombshell fell amongst us. But that was not the all of it. Apparently, Mr Bellamy (all lieutenants are called Mr) would not be content to just inspect our squad, he would be likely to speak to some of us as well. In other words, as he moved through the ranks making his inspection, he was going to single out some of us and ask us a question. The soldier who was thus addressed would immediately come smartly to attention, take one pace forward from the ranks and answer appropriately. Fortunately, the sarge had had advance notice of the penetrating questions Mr Bellamy was likely to ask. He had heard it all before. So we had the opportunity to be primed for this next challenge.

Apparently the most common question was,

'What's your name, soldier?'

This might not seem to pose too many problems, but we had to remember that it was necessary to snap one pace forward, slam to attention and shout out the correct reply, all at the same time.

But it might not be quite as simple as that. There were other questions he might ask. He could ask,

'What regiment do you belong to, soldier?'

or,

'Where are the regimental headquarters of your regiment, soldier?'

or,

'What is your Army number, soldier?'

or,

'Who is the Colonel-in-Chief of your regiment, soldier?'

So we were able to rehearse, with old sarge playing the part of Mr Bellamy and slurring out the questions.

The Army number was probably easier than the 'What's your name?' question, because we had now been in the Army long enough to talk about very little else. There was a certain religious significance to the Army number. Even within our squad we had a few recruits that had joined a few days later than our intake. We had numbers beginning 2333 . . . But there were a few Royal Fusiliers who were 2334 . . .'s and they were the subject of constant ridicule. Old Sloth Heath's number was 23336541. This meant that he had served at least two months longer than Webby and I and our lot. It is sad to relate that that was the only distinction Sloth ever achieved during his military service. And so, as every soldier knows his Army number like the back of his hand, this potential question held no fears for any of us.

There was a fair smattering of the squad in the Buffs. If we were asked in which regiment we served, we had two options for the reply. We could sing out,

'The Buffs, sir.'

Or we could say,

'The Third of Foot, sir.'

However, a little research showed us that Bellamy was in the Sussex Regiment and that the Sussex only rated as the Thirty-Fifth of Foot. It was pretty clear to all of the Buffs that, if we wanted to succeed in the Army, the prudent reply was 'The Buffs, sir'.

The Colonel of the Regiment is an honorary figure who assumes great importance to the regimental purists. Frequently some prominent Royal personage is the Colonel of the Regiment and, in the case of the Buffs, the Colonel of the Regiment was the King of Denmark.

There really should be no problems so long as Bellamy kept to the script.

However, dear old Sloth was the kind of person who only joined the Army to cause problems. Quite unwittingly he was about to make his little contribution. One of his many difficulties he faced in performing his current role as temporary, acting lance corporal was that he could not remember the names of the soldiers in his charge. Like Cpl Pru up the hill, acting corporal Sloth was in charge of one section of 95 Squad and he actually shared the barrack room with us. There were about eighteen beds in his room and he could not remember eighteen names. So he attached numbers to each of the beds to assist him in carrying out his duties. The Mole was bed No. 1, I was bed No. 2, Webby was bed No. 3 and so on around the freezing, derelict room.

The following day we 'fell in' on our own little section of the parade ground: best boots, No. 2 BD, Blanco all over the place. We were ready, but, nonetheless, Sarge gave us one more rehearsal, which passed without a hitch.

Suddenly, the impressive figure of Bomber Wells appeared from behind the cookhouse. He was accompanied by someone who looked very much like a boy of about twelve years of age. He wore a khaki peaked cap and he had a little yellow pip on each shoulder of his uniform. He was carrying a little leather swagger stick. Richard Todd he wasn't; this was 2nd Lt Bellamy.

Sgt Hastings leapt to attention.

'No. 95 Squad. AT TEN SHUN!' For once he didn't say 'Lishen to it', even though Baldwin was at least a second behind everyone else. 'Shlope arms!'

Sarge wheeled to his left and marched out on a spectacular arc as he approached the advancing hierarchy. One arm crashed to his side as he came to a blinding halt. This was followed by his very best salute.

'No. 95 Squad all preshent and ready for inspection, SHIR.'

Mr Bellamy gave a little wafty number in reply and advanced towards us with Bomber moving like a shadow at his side.

The tension gripped us, but we stood at attention, motionless.

Bellamy, with Bomber Wells glued to his side, started to saunter along the front rank about two feet in front of us. He stopped in front of Webby and pointed at him with his swagger stick.

'What's your Army number, soldier?'

Webby took a truly smart step forward.

'Three, sir,' he declared in a momentary aberration, confusing his Army number with Sloth's wretched bed numbers.

There was a look of stunned disbelief on Bellamy's face. Bomber Wells erupted.

'THREE! THREE! Blimey soldier you've seen some service. You must have been at bloomin' Agincourt!'

No one laughed. No one cried. We stood absolutely motionless hardly daring to breathe as Bellamy and Bomber continued to move along the line.

Almost inevitably they stopped opposite Baldwin. Again Bellamy waved his swagger stick indicating he was about to address Baldwin.

'What's your name, soldier?'

One pace forward and Baldwin was almost standing on Bellamy's foot.

'The King of Denmark, sir.'

8

STING LIKE A BUTTERFLY

All of these adventures had quite definitely been recorded
as part of the continuing process of assessment that was to
determine which of us would be candidates for Wozby. We
had been reliably informed that we were under constant
surveillance and every aspect of our daily activities would be
taken into account.

Just before being called up I had taken a driving test on a
small Vespa motor cycle. I had expected somehow that the
examiner would hop on the back in order to evaluate my
skills at first hand. In fact this was not the case. One reason
that the Ministry of Transport still has a few testers left is
because they don't in fact travel with the biker during the test.
I remember taking this very much to heart on my biker's test,
setting off with great attention to all aspects of the Highway
Code. At one point I had come to a correct halt at an intersec-
tion with a major road. In my stationary position I was giving
an elaborate hand signal indicating my intention to turn right,
when a policeman approached on foot to enquire whether I
had taken leave of my senses. I managed to convince him that
the examiner for my driving test was concealed near by and

would he kindly not interfere. I returned to the starting point of the test after an impeccable performance, spoilt only by a near arrest, but the tester was nowhere to be seen. I had presumed he was still making his way back from his spying position so was somewhat disappointed when he emerged from Sainsbury's carrying the week's shopping.

Life at Wemyss Barracks was not unlike taking the driving test on a bike. People assumed all sorts of postures that were struck entirely for the benefit of invisible assessors. Nowhere was this more apparent than in the daily routine of physical training. The Army puts great emphasis on anything to do with sports and things physical. Anyone with aspirations in the Army must be prepared to dive headlong over ditches, swing on ropes and generally excel in jungle activities. One place where this aptitude was tested daily was in the gymnasium under the gentle attention of the physical training staff.

The PL training camp had a large staff of physical training, or PE (physical education) instructors. They were given the rank of corporal. Their objective was to set impossible tasks in the gymnasium and then report who had failed to smile cheerfully as they went to their death. The instructors were issued with nice, warm, woolly, purple tracksuits. We performed in thin, red cotton T-shirts, black cotton shorts, that were first cousins of the Jungle Greens, and a pair of black (or brown if it rained and all the polish came off) gym shoes. The water in the red fire-buckets in the gymnasium was always frozen hard.

The PE instructors were notorious for a nice line in sadism, which usually effectively combined with a rather jaunty manner. Fortunately, most of our squad was fairly adept at leaping over walls and diving round obstacle courses. Even Baldwin could hold his own in the gymnasium. He had enormous strength in his upper body. This helped him when he returned to civilian life and became a rower of some renown. The instructors were quite wary of picking on Baldwin. They generally preferred to pick on smaller fry, which was why I jumped and bounced and ducked like a tormented grasshopper. From some of the other squads we heard some dreadful tales of the less athletic. Bodies were frequently left suspended from ropes, or trembling pitifully at some great height from where they were just incapable of jumping.

Many of the world's great athletes have tiny, piping voices. All Army PE instructors combine bulging muscles with the voice of a eunuch. Every exercise and every movement they demanded of us took the form of a competition.

'When I say "MOVE", I want to see the last man back to go three times around the gym, up the wall bars, over the vaulting horse, touch the fence across the other side of the parade ground and back again.'

'Are you ready? GO!' All squeaked in the voice of Alan Ball.

Off we go at a furious pace, crashing into one another in a desperate attempt to avoid being the last man back and suffer the consequences. Frozen, exhausted the last breathless few hurl themselves at the tape and collapse at the feet of the sadist, only to hear that little high-pitched voice saying,

'I didn't say "MOVE", I said, "GO". Now I say "MOVE!" '

Throughout every physical ordeal, it was absolutely essential to give the appearance of great determination and joy, otherwise the PE instructor might put in a report that there were some deficiencies in the leadership/utter stupidity department and one might as well kiss the old swagger-stick goodbye.

The head of the physical training department was a warrant officer of indeterminable age. He was tall and gaunt with a bald head, which made him look like a toffee apple. He was affectionately known as 'Rumpleforeskin'. He took great delight in making fleeting appearances at many of the tougher physical tests. He would, for instance, suddenly appear during a platoon cross-country race striding out ahead like a demented matchstick, with his sharp, bony knees bouncing up at stomach height. Then, after a brief spurt at the head of the column, he would stand to one side to urge everyone else along whilst uttering a stream of obscenities. Like so many of the training staff at the PL Headquarters, he was never seen without the inevitable clipboard. Even as he high-stepped on the cross country race, or those few hundred yards in which he participated, he would clutch his clipboard to his purple track suit and, as he stepped aside, he would always make a great show of jotting down comments about our respective performances. His vocabulary consisted of only a few four-letter words and his spelling of most of those was a bit doubt-ful. Nevertheless, the whole squad surged into overdrive if he was taking notes because we all knew that those reports on our keenness towards things physical carried a great deal of weight when the time came for decisions about who would be allowed to go to Wozby.

The Army loves all sports, but there is one sport, which towers over all others in importance in the eyes of the military. That sport is boxing. While other sports are highly regarded, the king of all sports in the Army is boxing. Boxing is manly and simply exudes leadership qualities. The Army can make a real meal out of an evening's boxing.

One day 95 and 96 Squads were lined up together and old Rumple himself strutted out in his purple tracksuit, which had three white stripes and a crown on the sleeve. It gave him great pleasure (you bet) to announce the forthcoming spectacular involving our two squads. In a week's time we would produce our best boxers to represent our two squads and we would fight against each other. The whole camp would attend and the officers would be there in full dress uniform. Furthermore, he could not emphasise too strongly, nor with more glee, how much our performance in that ring would count towards the assessment which would deter-mine whether we should be submitted to the Wozby Board.

Unfortunately, some of us would be disappointed because not everyone would be able to box, he said. Then he proceeded to read out the names of those who had earned selection, starting with the heavyweight division.

The competition in the super flyweight division was not too severe and, as I heard my name called out, I could hear myself saying this is BIG trouble.

I knew there was only one chance to survive this test, so I went straight to work. The man chosen to represent 96 Squad at my weight was called Moore. I vaguely remembered having seen this little fellow on parade and I had no difficulty picking him out in the NAAFI later that evening. I suggested a private meeting round the back of the cookhouse to discuss tactics. He very quickly seemed to see things the same way I did so all was very tidily arranged. We would put on a good show but, as he was only too pleased to agree, we would not do anything too drastic to one another. We even had a quick rehearsal. As a result I returned to my barrack room well satisfied that we could carry this off and I spent much of my spare time in the next week practising my dazzling footwork. Robin Berkeley had actually made a bit of a reputation as a boxer and he undertook to teach the rest of the team the first principles of the old Queensberry business.

The evening of the boxing competition came around rather quickly. On the night, the gymnasium was converted into Madison Square Garden. There was a raised podium in the middle of the gym and seating had been provided for the whole camp. Rows and rows of spectators lined the hall. Every warrant officer and NCO turned out in his best BD. The competitors sat in two little groups immediately opposite each other on either side of the ring. I caught the eye of 'Archie' Moore, as he had been named by the rest of 95 Squad, and he nodded knowingly. There was a sudden silence and then Bomber Wells jumped up and called the whole room to attention. In came the officers resplendent in their best dress uniforms, or Blues. The commanding officer, whom none of us had ever seen before, marched into his position in the front row of the tiered seats. He looked like every British actor I had ever seen winning the last war on the screen. Scrambled egg adorned his peaked Blues hat, his Sam Browne leather belt shone in the spotlights, which had been erected over the ring. He had his full array of medals pinned to his jacket. Behind him came a full complement of similarly dressed officers. I had no idea where they all came from. I could only think that, in deference to the occasion, someone had called Rent-an-Officer, or Madame Tussaud's.

But they were not the only ones in fancy dress, because there, before us in the ring, was the most incongruous sight of the evening. Old Rumpleforeskin was in the ring clutching a microphone. Instead of his purple tracksuit he wore an immaculate bow tie with his black dinner suit. His bald head glinted in the spotlight as he announced the rules of the competition. It was breathtaking to hear him sounding forth about THREE, THREE-MINUTE ROUNDS without once using the 'f' word. That was an indication of the importance of the occasion.

The first bout was the heavyweight division. Poor Simon Gillett had been chosen to represent our lot, reflecting his enormous height and fearsome appearance. The gentle philosopher was murdered.

There was a series of mismatches. Dreadful slaughter took place, but there was considerable heroism on the part of the vanquished. There was only one knock out, which was achieved by Robin Berkeley for our squad. His opponent took a very quick dismissal. The next contender representing 96 squad was David Ford.

I had run into David a few days before. We still had the same regime relating to the inspection of our white china mugs before each meal and, occasionally, some of the permanent NCOs would decide to carry out the inspection in order to enliven a dull evening. Whenever this happened there would be a long queue outside the quartermaster's stores the next day to replace the mugs that had not passed the inspection the evening before. As my mug had been one of the casualties, I was lining up to go into the store just as David was coming out. He was clutching a brand new mug. As he left the store he tripped over the step and the new mug crashed onto the concrete pathway. This meant he had to rejoin the queue to buy another one and so he and I had chatted a bit. In these rather inauspicious circumstances I met another brilliant soldier who would become a lifelong friend. Though we did not know it at the time, he and I would spend the rest of our service together.

But now David had to fight for his life. His opponent, representing our squad, was an absolute tiger called Richard Carr. He knew about boxing and he laid into David like a man possessed. I will never forget the fortitude with which David tried to contend. Even when his face began to look like last year's pudding, he continued to trade punches bravely with his tormentor.

After the bout Rumple announced the winner, but then he called for a special round of applause for a very game loser. The whole camp rose up and clapped David, even though he could not have been too aware of it at the time.

Suddenly I was in the ring. Rumple was back at the microphone,

'In the blue corner and representing 95 Squad . . .'

There wasn't much of a cheer, but a few of my mates in our squad managed a polite clap.

I sat on the lonely stool in my corner. I was accompanied by my second, who turned out to be one of the PE instructors I particularly disliked. I looked across the ring and nodded at my new mate from 96 Squad. As Rumple called out his name I distinctly saw him give me a wink.

The bell rang and my second took the first swing at me. I was completely stunned as he quite unexpectedly slammed a gum shield several sizes larger than my mouth between my teeth. He then shoved me forward into the ring.

I remembered that 'Archie' Moore had said to concentrate on the footwork in order to create a favourable impression, so I started my little dancing routine. Suddenly the lights went out.

I had been hit by such a flurry of leather that I could not open my eyes. For three minutes I reeled around the ring under a veritable barrage of uninterrupted blows to the face. I could see nothing but leather thudding into my eyes. This was definitely not what we had agreed upon.

Suddenly it stopped, but it took me a good time before I was able to reopen my eyes. When I did, I saw that my opponent was already sitting on his stool back in his corner. It then occurred to me that the bell must have gone to end the first round. In the cacophony of sound that was swirling around in my head, I had not particularly distinguished the sound of the bell. The bell had gone and I was slightly behind on points, but the only thing I could think about was this Judas who was in the ring with me, who had solemnly told me that he had no intention of doing anything other than going through the motions. I couldn't help wondering whose motions he thought he was going through. With this in mind I sat on my stool. My second flapped a towel in my face and gave me some encouragement.

'Crap,' he said.

The next two rounds followed the same pattern, until, suddenly, in the middle of the third round, there was another break in hostilities. This time I was sure the bell had not gone and I very nervously opened my remaining eye and peered out. Moore had reduced himself to such a state of exhaustion from his unsolicited attack that he had slipped. He was kneeling on one knee immediately in front of me. I summoned up every ounce of venom within me and struck him a mighty blow as he knelt defenceless before me.

The lecture from the referee was deeply hurtful. Hitting a man when he is down is in contravention of old Queensberry rules and the referee was required to deduct a penalty point from my score. However, he very pointedly said he could not make the mandatory deduction because, on his scorecard, I had not yet scored a single point for him to deduct.

When Rumple announced the result, which incidentally decided the whole match in favour of 96 Squad, there was no reference to a gallant loser.

9

PANAMA AND OTHER PARADES

The daily morning parade of all of the PL platoons was a major event. It offered the opportunity for most of the cast of characters to shine and there was no shortage of characters at Wemyss Barracks.

Sgt Major 'Bomber' Wells was the dominant character of the entire camp and he presided over every morning parade, always immaculate, always in charge and, occasionally, showing flashes of Sussex humour.

There were about two hundred and fifty PLs but the total population of Wemyss Barracks was about twice that number. For every PL under training there was at least one other soldier doing something or other to keep the camp ticking over. Apart from the training staff, consisting of the sergeant major and his staff of training sergeants, the weapons training instructors and the PE instructors, there was another whole Army called the Permanent Staff. Nobody really knew how many there were, or what they actually did, but there are a lot of these unsung heroes in the Army. There are cooks, clerks and storemen; there are drivers, mechanics and medics; there are Military Police, Signals and maintenance men. There is a great assembly of skilled men, whose principal aim is to avoid doing anything which resembles the actual business of soldiering. Some of this great crowd of skivers and layabouts achieved legendary levels of skills when it came to the avoidance of military duties. A good infantryman is taught to treat his rifle as wife, friend and lover all rolled into one. It was remarkable how many soldiers could develop the same affection for a broom or a shovel.

A broom or a shovel was indispensable if one was fortunate enough to be on the Permanent Staff. Either of these trusty friends, provided it was judiciously combined with the appearance of either just starting or just finishing some important task, was a better friend than the old crooked shooter. There were hordes of soldiers wandering around the camp in dirty fatigues and clutching a broom or a shovel. Occasionally they would stop for a rest and move the fag from one side of the mouth to the other and this seemed to be their only contribution to the war effort.

Most of the Permanent Staff was not permanent at all. They were national servicemen who were coming to the end of their two years' service. They somehow managed to form a sort of fifth column outside the discipline that grabbed everyone else in the camp. To be a fully paid up member of this column one had to show almost total apathy towards all aspects of the military existence except the ending of it. As the end of their service approached, they were able to make their supreme contribution to life in the camp by rejoicing at the passing of each minute of their remaining time. This was displayed in a number of different ways. The most conventional was simply to shout out to anyone and everyone the number of days remaining before demob. While the training squads were being hounded around the parade ground, somewhere in the background there would almost always be a cry of, 'Six weeks, Four days, Two hours, Seventeen minutes and an Early Breakfast!'

On the day of demob a soldier was permitted the option to take an early breakfast so he could catch his train home. This cry would echo all over the camp at various times of the day or night and would serve as a reminder to us that we had at least twenty months to serve before any of us would taste an 'early breakfast'.

Not content with shouting out the remaining time to serve, these soldiers, who had developed a medical condition known as 'Demob Happy', would cover the camp in graffiti celebrating their imminent release. In the cookhouse was a blackboard that was supposed to be used by the cooks to inform us of the menu, because much of the food was not immediately recognisable. But it was always covered in patterns that were known as 'gloat charts' or 'chuff charts':

> Grin Pee Soup
> Sosseches & Spud
> Puding 5 Days To Go

This would usually appear as a series of dashes or lines to represent the unexpired units of time. These were then rubbed out or crossed off as the time elapsed. It was not unknown to see the whole two years of someone's national service divided into minutes and then religiously ticked off minute by minute. No ancient wall in the historic city of Canterbury escaped unscathed.

One of the other achievements of these soldiers was that they were excused from attending the morning parade. The official reason given was that their other duties were so important and so arduous that they could not be prejudiced by time-consuming appearances on the parade. But everyone knew that the real reason was that these awful soldiers were beyond redemption and would destroy the Bomber's parade if they were allowed to attend.

As well as the so-called Permanent Staff, the broom and shovel brigade, there was another group alongside the PLs. This group was called headquarters platoon and they were required to parade along with us each day. This group, also mainly consisting of national servicemen, had almost fallen in clover. Some rather spurious claims to numeracy or literacy had enabled them to aspire to office duties. They 'worked' in the sergeant major's own office. Here they either typed out company notices, or they pinched the petrol or fiddled the payroll.

Headquarters platoon was led by one of Wemyss Barracks' true warriors. His name was Cpl Lewis. Cpl Lewis was the scion of one of the country's prominent Roman Catholic families. He had been educated at a great and famous Jesuit College in the Midlands and had then completed three years at Oxford University where he had achieved distinction as a scholar and a poet. Before he was able to fulfil his destiny as a highborn Catholic Priest, he had been nabbed by HM to do his national service. He had himself once been a PL and had made an appearance before the Wozby board. The board was quite unable to classify this divine character and decided to defer him in the category called 'Watch'. He had duly returned to Wemyss Barracks and had stayed there ever since. He was an aesthete and an aristocrat, though he proved himself to be a lousy soldier. But, in spite of this, he had been promoted to full corporal and put in charge of HQ platoon. Sgt Major Wells had a penchant for whiling away the time between parades by doing crossword puzzles and he needed Lewis at hand to help him with some of the more esoteric clues. The only time I had to attend the sergeant major's office on a small disciplinary matter, I waited outside and listened to a typical exchange,

'Fifteen down. Seven f . . . ing letters. Bloomin' Adriatic setting. Twelfth f . . . ing Night. F . . . ing blank, f . . . ing Y, f . . . ing blankety blank and ending in A,' called out Bomber.

'Illyria,' I called out, before I had time to remember where I was.

The door to the sergeant major's office opened and Cpl Lewis marched me in to the office at the double.

'Left, Right, Left, Right. Halt, Smartarse,' rather as though he was chanting a Te Deum.

When not sitting in front of the warm fire in the sergeant major's office Cpl Lewis would circle the parade ground on a rusty old bicycle. While the fearsome training sergeants were drilling their platoons, Lewis would weave erratically around them. Sometimes he would even whistle in between the sergeant and the platoon he was drilling, but nobody ever objected to Cpl Lewis' eccentric behaviour. He was forgiven because of his patrician manners, his delightful sense of humour and his closeness to Bomber Wells.

'Morning, Lewis,' growls the sergeant.

'Morning, Ducky,' and the bicycle flies onwards.

The squad, which paraded immediately behind ours, was No. 96 Squad. The squad included David Ford. Their training sergeant was called Sgt Morrish. The first time we had heard the name was when he was greeted by our sergeant, Sgt Hastings, old 'Lishen to It'. Naturally we assumed that 96 Squad's sergeant was called Morris, but, just to confuse everyone, it turned out that his name really was Morrish. Because Morrish lined up on parade in front of his squad and I was the back man in our squad, I became a candidate for the colourful language that was Sgt Morrish's hallmark.

'Stand still, the bow-legged dwarf in the rear!'

He had a very peculiar moustache that he obviously thought gave him the appropriate parade ground credentials, but, in fact, it made him look like a mix between Hitler and Salvador Dali. He adored the obscenities of the parade ground. In later life he might well have written the script for most of the 'Carry On' movies.

'An' I'll put my boot so far up your arse you'll spit Cherry Blossom for a month!' The voice rising on every word to reach a crescendo.

All the members of 96 Squad went around with completely shaven heads, to prevent a cry from Morrish,

''Air cut. Get your fockin' 'air cut. It's so long I'm standing on it!'

Any soldier whose position, when standing to attention, allowed a glimmer of daylight through their legs was inevitably charmed with,

'Close your legs, your breath smells!'

No. 96 Squad included in its ranks a real rarity. This rarity was a recruit called David Herbert. He was a rarity because he had been a choirboy at Westminster Abbey and had sung at the Coronation of Queen Elizabeth. After the ceremony HM had issued a coronation medal which was awarded to all those service personnel who had played any part in the ceremony. Not only was this awarded to the Household Cavalry, who had accompanied the Queen down the Mall, but also to all the policemen who had lined the route and, according to David Herbert, all choristers if they were subsequently called up. No one seemed to challenge this claim and Herbert had stitched the colourful little ribbon, denoting the award, on to his BD just above his left breast pocket on his tunic.

Quite a lot of the regular soldiers wore campaign medals, or the little strip of ribbon that denoted same, on their uniform. Those who were too young to put in an appearance in the Second World War could have picked up ribbons from Kenya, Korea or Palestine. So there was no shortage of colour splashed amongst the training sergeants, but there wasn't exactly a rainbow around the squads of PLs. Since the only action we had seen was one minor fracas in the ablutions and, since most of us had not yet seen three months' service, it was slightly incongruous to see a PL wearing a medal. And it made David Herbert a marked man. As we all lined up on the big parade ground, Bomber Wells would navigate by reference to Herbert.

'You, with the VC!' Or, 'the man behind/to the left/right

of the man with the VC'. After a few weeks of daily parades Herbert was regretting his distinction.

Every day all the squads lined up on the parade ground in sequence, the senior squad at the front. Each training sergeant would parade in front of his own squad and the acting lance corporals would fall in with their respective squad. HQ platoon, under the stirring command of Cpl Lewis, would fall in at the rear, behind all of the PL squads. When all the sergeants were satisfied that everyone was shipshape, they would position themselves, rigidly to attention, immediately in front of their squad. When everyone was in position, Sgt Major Wells would enter stage left, where he was the focus of attention. Moustaches bristling, leather shining and with the sergeant major's pace stick tucked under his arm, he would sweep on to the parade ground and come to a resounding halt. Then he would call out the number of each squad in turn.

'Numbah Nointy-Two Squad!'

Back comes the reply,

'Nointytwosquadallpresentandcorrect. Ready for inspection, Sah!'

The same exchange would take place with 93 Squad, then with 94 Squad and so on. Finally, we would reach HQ platoon and prepare for the piping voice and perfect diction of Cpl Lewis. His reply was always different from all the training sergeants of the PL squads. Poor old Lewis always had a litany of disasters to report.

'Headquarters platoon,' piped up Lewis, followed by a long pause. 'One man sick, one man AWOL (deserter), one man on Jankers (locked in the guardroom), otherwise all present and ready for inspection, sir.'

'Wot's matter with the one man sick, Cpl Lewis?' called out the sergeant major.

'Acne, sir.'

''Ackney? I thought that was a bloomin' carriage. Wot the

'ell is wrong with 'im?' called out Sgt Major Wells across the whole parade ground to Cpl Lewis some fifty yards away.

Across the crisp November morning air wafted Lewis' immortal reply, 'Spotty Botty, sir.'

There was always drama on the morning parade. One day we completed the regular opening ceremony with Lewis giving graphic details of the latest disasters to overtake HQ platoon, when Bomber Wells announced a most unusual development. He told us that the commanding officer himself was going to come on to the parade and address us. When the CO arrived, he was accompanied by the whole complement of the camp's officers. They marched onto the parade ground and then stood rather awkwardly behind the colonel. This was serious stuff. 'Must be war,' muttered someone in the ranks beside me, under his breath.

The CO returned Bomber's salute and then marched briskly towards us. He stopped a few paces in front of the senior squad and then waved his leather stick around a couple of times. Within a few seconds it was clear that the soldier who had whispered 'It must be war', was right on the button. The colonel told us that that same morning another colonel, called Nasser, had helped himself to one of our canals without so much as a by your leave. The whole camp was to be put on a state of high alert and we were to be watchful for any threats of enemy action. The guard was to be doubled and sentries would be posted around the camp day and night.

We had not seen many Egyptians when we had ventured into the ancient city of Canterbury, but, nevertheless, a little wave of excitement and anticipation ran through the ranks as Colonel Bradley broke the news to us. But this was not all.

The colonel continued his address by telling us that there was a distinct possibility that we (the Brits, that is) might declare war and invade Egypt to get our canal back. In this case it was possible that we might be hurled into action.

He said that he had heard from the War Office that, even though we had not yet completed our basic training, we were on standby. He then marched off the parade ground, leaving us to ponder our fate. Was it possible that we might find ourselves, including Baldwin, thrown into combat?

We were brought down to earth by the gentle Sussex voice of the sergeant major,

'Right, you lot. You all heard what the officer said. Now get a grip. You could be lucky enough to be amongst the shock troops. I don't know about the fockin' Gippos, but, by God, you would shock me! And now go back to your duties and pray to the Almighty that we can get back our Panama Canal. Dismiss.'

10

THE WOZZER

The Suez Canal was recaptured without any contribution from 95 Squad. However, when the British lads finally reached the canal, they found that the Egyptians had clogged it up with old bricks and sunken ships. When more details of the events leading up to the engagement became known, the whole enterprise took on a distinctly off-colour hue. After Nasser had seized the canal, the British Government dithered before taking action. After a while the Israelis took advantage of the uncertainty and launched an attack on Egypt. Then the British, with their allies, the French, sent off their expeditionary force on the pretext that they were peacemakers and were seeking to separate the warring parties. The Americans were thoroughly dissuaded by this argument and sought to deter the Brits by a devastating attack, not on the fighting men of 95 Squad, but on the poor old defenceless Pound Sterling. It subsequently became known that the Brits and the French had colluded with the Israelis and encouraged them to attack Egypt, using that attack as an excuse to intervene and regain control of the Suez Canal.

At the time of our military intervention, the atmosphere

amongst non-participating servicemen was one of high idealism. In the unlikely event that we had come across any Egyptians skulking in the cloisters around Canterbury Cathedral, I have no doubt, whatsoever, that we would have attempted to inflict the most awful damage upon them. How often have young men in uniform honourably pursued a military campaign totally oblivious of the degree of dishonour to which their politicians were exposing them?

In any event we needed a new Prime Minister after this little fiasco.

But the PLs down Canterbury way soldiered on. We were outwardly frustrated to have missed this little piece of action, but, if we were truly honest, we knew we were nowhere near ready for action. We were pretty good with Blanco and Brasso, but had not had much experience with the Lee Enfield and had only once been on the range with the Bren gun. Furthermore, Egypt was a 'hot' country and this war would have been fought in our jungle greens and we all knew what crippling limitations these imposed on a fighting man.

The world was such an uncertain place in those days. We may have missed one little war, but you could be pretty sure that there would be another one coming along fairly soon, just like a London bus. So we carried on with our training and progressed slowly towards our destiny, the mother of all confrontations, our meeting with the War Office Selection Board, or the Big Wozzer.

Every two weeks one of the squads ahead of us disappeared. Most of them went off to WOSB. But we never learned much about their fate. It was difficult to get much feedback on their results. The successful ones never came back because they went straight off to officer cadet school. The unsuccessful ones never came back because they were returned to their units (RTU). The only ones to come back among us were those who made up the amorphous group who neither passed nor failed but were deferred 'Watch'. Generally these were not terribly reliable witnesses when it came to relating the fate of their colleagues. Often, they simply did not know which of their colleagues had passed or failed. There were rumours of the most terrible massacres. A man who rejoiced in the name of Gordon Bennett, who returned under the 'Watch' category, swore that his entire squad had failed and that he was the only one to survive to tell the tale. Apparently, the board handed out pretty summary justice and groups were dispersed without any opportunity to compare notes. Immediately after the selections were made, everyone was rapidly disbanded and transported wherever they went next.

So we were kept in a fairly high state of anxiety as our own examination approached. Not only did we not know what the success rate had been in the squads that had gone before, we did not really know what qualities we were supposed to display. It wasn't like any previous exam we had ever taken. Most of us had a fair idea what was required to pass an A-level, not that that meant we had all passed them all, but at least we were aware of the curriculum and the standards that were generally expected. But here this WOSB thing was just a great leap in the dark. In the three months we had been in the Army we had hardly had any contact with any commissioned officers. We had been inspected once by our own platoon officer, 2nd Lt Bellamy, but conversation on that occasion had been somewhat limited. Strangely, even though I did not know it then, the subject of the King of Denmark was going to raise its ugly head again at my own WOSB.

We were trained almost exclusively by NCOs. Most of them were good professional soldiers, but to them it was inconceivable that their Army would even consider taking any of this part-time rabble and try to turn them into commissioned officers. Certainly they were not in a position to give us any guidance as to how to conduct ourselves before the board.

Truthfully, we did not know whether the examining board would be judging us on our table manners or on our fighting spirit. All we did know was that the whole process took three days and that we would have to report to a mystery destination somewhere near Andover.

When our turn came, most of our squad was deemed competent to be submitted to the board. We were carefully split up so that none of us would actually be tested together. We were all given different dates and different times to report to Wozby.

Once again I found myself travelling full of trepidation on a train. Once again, I was met by a sergeant with a clipboard when I arrived at Andover station. Once again, I was loaded into a three-ton truck and looked nervously at my fellow passengers. But, this time, no cheerful Webby, no Grandad Farrar, no Jumbo, just a load of complete strangers. These were all candidates to present themselves to the board. We were all national servicemen and we had been drawn from all parts of the country. There was a huge Scotsman from the Highland Light Infantry (HLI), a rather pucker chap from the Coldstream Guards, one from the Glosters, one from the Manchester Regiment and others who sat in such a way that I could not read their little regimental shoulder flashes. There were about a dozen hopefuls all destined to go through their paces the next day. Everyone behaved in a thoroughly gentlemanly way, but there was a marked undertone to the rather forced conversation in the truck. The conversation itself was pleasant enough but it was clear that we were trying to weigh each other up as we were all slightly in competition with each other.

My memory of the next three days is imperfect. We formed a little squad of just eight men and for the next three days we slept in the same hut, ate in the same canteen and vied with each other in our attempts to impress a variety of different officers with our leadership qualities. There were tests of stamina, tests of initiative, interviews, discussion panels and even speeches. I can only remember a determination to display, at all times, a great enthusiasm and spirit which, I thought, might be mistaken for officer-like qualities. I was most perturbed by the differing interpretation which others in the group put upon the mysterious leadership qualities. The chap in the Coldstream Guards went off in completely the opposite direction. He spent three days displaying an attitude of enormous natural superiority. While I rushed around from test to test, he hardly deigned to move himself at all. During one of the discussion panels he asked the examining officer if he might smoke and then lit up a large cigar and talked about Boodles.

Throughout the three days we were under the constant supervision of a quiet-spoken captain in the Parachute Regiment. He remained in attendance wherever we went. There was also a very cheerful corporal who marched us from place to place. Most of us called him 'sir' or 'Corporal'. But the chap in the Coldstream Guards called him 'My good man', which impressed us enormously. And all the time the captain in the Paras watched.

There were several interviews with rows of imposing officers. During one of my interviews, a full colonel in the Suffolk Regiment noted that I was in the Buffs and asked me about the Colonel of the Regiment. I seized on this as a gift question and yelled out, 'The King of Denmark, sir!' This was greeted with a singularly bemused expression from the members of the panel and particularly from the colonel who had asked the question. It turned out that he had some old crony who was a colonel in the Buffs and he was asking me if I knew him. When I finally understood the question, I had to admit that I had not mixed with many senior officers in the Buffs during my basic training at Howe Barracks. I tried to pull the fat out of the fire by referring to Cpl Prudence, but the colonel in the Suffolks seemed to lose interest.

The most demanding leadership tests were conducted by Captain Inscrutable. He set our group of eight a series of tasks and we each took it in turn to take command and complete the task. This all required a fertile imagination because most of the projects involved crossing a river, usually carrying wounded men and various weapons, while the enemy, usually represented by our cheerful corporal, launched a series of vicious attacks. Since the only props we had were a few poles and an old ammunition box, the whole scene bordered on the comic. But in spite of these limitations everyone was trying desperately to show off his own idea of officer-like attitudes.

If our captain had not been quietly observing our every move and taking notes on his clipboard and, if this exam had not been the single most important thing we had encountered in our entire lives, this might have been quite an entertaining diversion. As it was, it produced some of the most frenetic and fearless activity ever seen in the greater Andover area. Our group quickly came to revolve around the huge Scotsman in the HLI and the little man from the Buffs. Each task involved men climbing on top of each other to form a bridge over an imaginary obstacle. Each successful commander would attempt to outdo all the others with the precision of his commands.

Always the poor Scotsman would be ordered to act as the base to a huge and disorganised pyramid of bodies. Then, just as he was creaking under the weight of three colleagues, two wounded soldiers and a twenty-five pound artillery piece, the temporary commander would shout,

'Right. Now, where's the little man? Where's the little bugger in the Buffs?'

'Right, there you are. Now, I want you to carry that ammunition box and climb over that wounded chap and get up on the shoulders of those other guys. Then swing across the . . . Oh, S . . . t! Look out . . .'

Every time the whole group would collapse in a heap in the

imaginary river with poles and wounded comrades flying in all directions.

After the first three attempts there was no longer any need to simulate a wounded comrade. The poor guardsman had nearly been fatally injured in one of the collapses, but he heroically carried on assuming the wounded soldier role in a thoroughly stoical and upper-class way.

Meanwhile, this constant climbing to the peak gave me adequate opportunity to impress with my tremendous enthusiasm. Time and again I responded to the hopelessly misguided commands of my colleagues. With almost total disregard for my own safety, I leapt into action, scrambling up the back of the long-suffering Scotsman and crashing cheerfully to the ground, smiling inanely at the captain all the time.

My own project, when it was my turn to assume command, was by far the most complicated. Old Captain Stiff Upper was letting his imagination run away with him. By the time it was my turn the river had apparently come into full flood. What's more I had to contend with a wounded man, a heavy artillery piece and an elephant. I had to get all of these across the raging torrent. Furthermore, it was tersely pointed out to me that the enemy, who were described as a bunch of 'ferocious Fuzzy Wuzzies', were closing in fast and were notorious for some fighting practices which fell well short of the minimum standards of the Geneva Convention.

I have since learned that one of the qualities which is deemed necessary to make an officer is a sense of urgency. My own urgency might more accurately be described as total panic. I screamed orders at the poor Scot. I told the wounded guardsman to pull his f . . . ing finger out and generally ran around like a demented dervish. Finally, I had poles, Scotsman and the elephant all suspended in mid-air when I completely lost my head. In desperation for an extra pair of hands, I yelled at the captain himself,

'Don't just stand there. Give that man a hand with that elephant!'

The captain, who had never been known to even smile up to that point, broke into a broad grin. Apparently, he interpreted this as a piece of real initiative.

Other tests included making a three-minute speech to the rest of the group and a panel of officers. I chose to speak about my experiences as a preparatory school master. Whilst waiting to be called up, I had worked for two terms as a teacher of Spotted Dicks in Remove at two separate prep schools. I had been given subjects to teach, about which I had no more than a passing acquaintance and I had had to run fast to keep ahead of the inevitable little smart-asses. I very much doubt if I taught them anything but I certainly learned from the experience and I managed to keep myself out of Carey Street. It also provided me with the ideal subject for my three-minute speech. As a matter of fact, I might have gone on for much longer because teaching at a prep school was the second most absurd thing I had done in my life. I was able to recall several jolly incidents with which to regale the examining board.

I ended my speech, saluted smartly and moved back to join the group. As I did so I heard one of the board whisper to a colleague,

'Jolly little fellah. What!'

I just could not work out whether this was good or bad. Did the Army want to give the Queen's commission to 'jolly little fellows'? I continued to puzzle this out while listening to the wounded guardsman give his three-minute dissertation on 'Riding to hounds'.

I don't recall all the other tests to which we were subjected, but I do remember the last test of all, which was a sort of grand finale. This was the most fiendish obstacle course ever devised by the British Army. It comprised every obstacle known to man and was as much a test of strength and stamina as of agility. There was barbed wire to crawl over, huge walls to scale, miles of camouflage netting to crawl under and a massive water jump, straight out of the Grand National. Just to make sure this was not too simple, we had to attempt the obstacle course wearing a steel helmet and full battle gear. All the while, Captain Strong-Silent-Type stood a few paces away quietly making notes on his bloody clipboard.

Our first competitor was the nice young guy from the Glosters. Up to this point he had been a slightly anonymous member of the group and I got the feeling that he was aware that so far he had probably not made much of an impression. The Glosters might have been the heroes of Korea, but this particular Gloster had had a fairly quiet Wozby to date.

He was, clearly, utterly determined to make his mark on this final test. He set off at the water jump like Fanny Blankers-Koen, arms waving, boots pounding over the undergrowth. He accelerated up the hill and approached the huge water jump at a totally unsustainable pace. Just before take-off, his tin hat slipped and fell forward over his eyes. He used radar to guess the point at which to launch himself into the air, but his radar deceived him utterly and he leapt about two feet too soon, so that he landed right in the middle of the water.

It quickly became clear from the spluttering and gasping that the long jump was not the only event at which he did not excel. His swimming also left quite a lot to be desired and a very long time elapsed with only minor parts of his body visible. Soon even these began to disappear from view and Captain Clipboard began to look a mite concerned.

I wasn't born yesterday, or the day before. I knew a chance to impress when I saw one. Before any one else could take the God-given opportunity, I flung off my own tin hat and dived in to the rescue. With total disregard for my own safety, but with one eye on the clipboard, I struggled through the water to bring the Gloster Regiment to safety. All the others in the group rushed to help, apart from the guardsman, who viewed the whole episode with total disdain. But it was too late. Not that the poor chap had drowned, just that they had all missed the golden opportunity to pass the initiative test.

When my own turn to attempt the obstacle course came, I received the most sympathetic treatment from the captain. I managed to leap the water, climb the huge wall, crawl under the netting, but then I came to the part where I had to lift a weighted ammunition box over a parallel bar. I summoned up my last ounce of energy, but only managed to lift the box about half way to the parallel bar. For most of the larger fellows the bar was a little over waist height. For me, it was more like shoulder height and I just knew that no amount of heaving was going to get this heavy box up to the bar. After several abortive attempts my snatch-and-jerk technique was producing diminishing returns.

'Never mind, laddie. You can leave that. You've already done really well.' The captain had walked over and was actually patting me on the shoulder.

Out of the corner of my eye I could see the rest of the group staring at me. Hatred and envy were equally balanced in their collective expression.

11

EATON HALL

There are really two different armies. There are the real fighting men and there are the rest. The fighting men are called the infantry, or, sometimes, the PBI, or Poor Bloody Infantry. These are the chaps you have seen on British Movietone News storming up the Normandy beaches or engaged in hand to hand fighting in the desert. This Army had an officer cadet school called Eaton Hall, which was just outside Chester.

But there was another Army as well and it had its own officer cadet school called Mons, which was near Aldershot. Mons took Gunners and Tanks, Signals and Sappers, Cooks and Mechanics, REME (Royal Electrical and Mechanical Engineers), RASC (Royal Army Service Corps), Royal Artillery, Pay Corps, Signals. These and many others went to Mons, while the real Army went to Eaton Hall. The dividing line between Eaton Hall and Mons was exactly how one went into battle. Those that did not go into battle at all automatically went to Mons. Those that went into battle on their own two feet went to Eaton Hall, but anyone who went into battle in a tank or on a horse or some other sissy form of transport would go to Mons.

* * *

Just outside the beautiful City of Chester was a Gothic pile that used to be home to the Dukes of Westminster. This Victorian mausoleum had been widely recognised as the ugliest building in Europe and it was noteworthy that the then Duke of Westminster had not protested too loudly when the British Government had expropriated the whole complex during the war.

The buildings included vast reception halls and chambers that had once been ballrooms and libraries. The Army had converted these to other uses such that we were to practise weapon training and drill in the most incongruous surroundings. The main palace (The Palace of Westminster?) sported a clock tower that was a sort of caricature of Big Ben. This also was converted to our use. The officer cadet school at Eaton Hall had the highest suicide rate in the country and the Tower seemed to have a macabre fascination for many of the poor young men who could not cope with the pressures of their time at Eaton Hall.

The Army had complemented these appalling buildings with its own particular trademarks. Grafted on to the Victorian architecture was an array of camouflage, barbed wire, asphalt and Nissen huts that elevated the whole mess into superstar status in the annals of unsightliness and left the whole pile suitable only to serve as an officer cadet school or a mental institution. Any cadet with the slightest sensitivity to his immediate surroundings would join the queue at the top of the tower.

But the real attraction of Eaton Hall to the Army was the huge forecourt, which made the ideal parade ground. We were to spend four months at Eaton Hall and, at the end of that period, those that had survived this most arduous training would take part in a passing-out parade. This would be the culmination of all our efforts. Passing-out parades are to the Army what the last night is to Promenade Concerts. It is the be-all and end-all, a triumph, a celebration and a graduation all rolled into one. A passing-out parade at an officer cadet school – Sandhurst, Dartmouth, Cranwell, Eaton Hall or even Mons – is a BIG event. Parents in morning dress, field marshals, dukes and princesses all show up at passing-out parades. In fact it was not all that unusual for HM herself to take the salute as she does each year at Trooping the Colour. Quite often there have been kings and dukes in the ranks as well. The Duke of Kent had struck a fine figure at Sandhurst just before our time at Eaton Hall.

One of the most memorable cries across any parade ground had been directed across the parade ground at Sandhurst to King Hussein of Jordan,

'You, sir, king, sir. Move your feet sharpish, sir. You are the idlest king on this parade, sir!'

For these and all other parades the vast forecourt at Eaton Hall was Manna from Heaven. It was a vast semicircle of marching area. The whole college could parade on this forecourt and still leave room for a couple of military bands and Regimental Sergeant Major D. T. Lynch, DCM. In one corner of the parade ground was a huge statue of one of the long-forgotten Dukes of Westminster in full regalia recalling an appearance as a substitute at the battle of Waterloo. He was mounted on a massive steed, slightly reminiscent of the one that used to do the coal round when I was a boy. The horse stood in the middle of a round pond.

Just before our little crowd arrived at Eaton Hall, there had been a passing-out parade that secured a special place in military history. Veterans of this particular parade still talk of the achievements of that day over forty years later.

Some of the cadets, who were to graduate on that day, had discovered that the whole statue was hollow. At dead of night, before the parade, they had removed the Duke's plumed hat, borrowed the camp fire engine and filled the statue with two hundred gallons of water. They had then pricked a small hole in the very tip of the horse's huge member, which they filled with wax. The wax was timed to dissolve at the very moment that Princess Margaret marched on to the parade ground to take the salute. At precisely the right moment the horse started to relieve himself noisily into the surrounding pond and continued without interruption for twenty-four hours.

There were four companies of officer cadets at Eaton Hall. After lengthy deliberation the War Office had come up with highly imaginative names for the four companies. They were called A, B, C and D Coy. Each company was divided into two platoons and these carried the same theme to even greater heights and were called 1 and 2 platoons.

I found that I was to be in No. 1 Platoon in A Coy, which seemed to have a nice ring to it. Not only did it have a nice ring but also I was overwhelmed to find a few famil-iar faces. Our first day at Eaton Hall turned out to be yet another old girls' reunion. In my platoon was old Grandad Farrar himself; Jumbo Fuller was there and so was dear Tony Swinson. In No. 2 Platoon, which was housed in the next Nissen hut, was the Mole limbering up to play rugby, cricket and hockey all at once. Webby had passed WOSB as well, but, for some unknown reason, he joined B Coy just behind us, where he was caught up by several members of 96 Squad from Canterbury, including David Ford who has yet to play a starring role in this story.

But now we had been joined by cadets who were drawn from different regiments from all over the country. There were men from the Rifle Brigade who had double-barrelled names and green berets. There were Gurkhas and Marines. There was a guardsman called Courtauld. There were Scotsmen in the Camerons and Welshmen in the Welch [sic] Regiment. There were Buffs and Staffs, there were Suffolks and Surreys, Queen's and King's Own; we had Beds and Herts and Yorks and Lancs, Manchester and Devons, Coldstreamers and Grenadiers.

There was the most fearsome man I had ever seen dressed in a kilt, the biggest, darkest soldier imaginable who was appropriately serving in the Black Watch. He looked like a mix between Macbeth and the huge competitor in the Highland Games who used to appear on the back of the porridge packet. His name was Philip Howard and he had already completed a distinguished career at Oxford University where he had combined playing outstanding rugby with achieving a first class degree. He also showed himself over the next weeks to be an excellent soldier and was appointed one of the under-officers, or stick orderlies, for our passing-out parade. This huge man's delicate touch with the English language adorns the pages of *The Times* to this day.

There was yet another of the Mole's old school friends in A Coy. His name was 'Bertie' Bois and he was totally disreputable in a quiet and likeable way. He had originally joined the Regular Army and had gone to Sandhurst. But unfortunately his singular commitment to good wine and bad women had proved too much even for that institution which was renowned for its leniency in that area. He had returned to pursue the same interests in civilian life, which were only interrupted when he was subjected to the greatest of ironies; he was called up to do his national service. But he was to have the last laugh because the Wozby Board was not deterred by his previous Army record or by his beautifully flippant attitude and here he was at another officer cadet school preparing to secure the Queen's commission after all.

Bertie might also have been a fine athlete and, in particular, a rugby player at the highest level if his constant pursuit of other pleasures had not intervened. He was selected to play for the Eaton Hall XV, which, at that time, was one of the strongest teams in the country. Gordon Waddell, who would shortly captain Scotland and David Perry, who would be captain of England, were both contemporaries of ours at Eaton Hall. A place in the rugby team virtually guaranteed a commission. But

Bertie inadvertently lit up a cigarette in the scrum during a vital game and had to leave the field under a cloud.

Another man in our platoon had arrived in a brand new Austin Healey sports car, which was the envy of the whole camp. His name was 'Butch' Mackenzie Hill and he also was no slouch around the bar. On one occasion, after a spell of heavy frontline duty in Chester, he only just returned to camp in time for the morning parade. A Coy was already preparing to line up and fall-in when a blue and white Austin Healey shot across the parade ground and came to rest in a hedge just outside our Nissen hut. Officer Cadet Mackenzie Hill leapt out dressed in a spotted silk dressing gown. He was seen to disappear into our Nissen hut and reappear in full battledress in less than a minute and took his place in the ranks.

'Sorry I'm late, sir. Secret mission, sir. Fog on manoeuvres, sir!'

Butch went on to be the undisputed middleweight champion of the Cambridge University boxing team and then, in the 1970s, he built up the largest private company in Britain only to be tragically struck down with cancer at only fifty years of age.

Martin Baldwin had not made it through Wozby this time, but we had a more than adequate substitute. His name was Larry Shore and he was a Glorious Gloster. Larry brought a new dimension to uncoordination. He was a perfectionist. His particular speciality was an inability to separate right from left, a characteristic which fitted him out well for a career later in British Rail. Like me, he was a fairly small man, which meant that he and I would march side by side at the rear of our platoon. Any command involving either right or left was a challenge to poor Larry Shore. Either the whole platoon would turn smartly one way and Larry would turn directly in to me, or we would all smartly turn left and Larry would turn right and detach himself from the rest of us, marching off on his own into the distance like the lone legionnaire.

* * *

We had not to this point in our Army careers had any contact with the Brigade of Guards. The Guards were exclusive, like a little Army within the Army. They did not train alongside us at Wemyss Barracks. All their basic training was carried out at the Guards Depot at Caterham and, by all accounts, this was the toughest basic training in the British Army. The Guards are an elite corps. Their standards are higher than any other section of the Army and nowhere is this more in evidence than on the parade ground. No one can watch the Trooping the Colour or the changing of the guard outside Buckingham Palace and not see it is self evident that the Guards are just in a different league.

The Guards' officers are peacocks from the aristocracy, the guardsmen are tougher and smarter than any others in the Army, but the most famous representatives of the Brigade of Guards are their sergeant majors.

The Guards ran Eaton Hall. The commanding officer was Colonel B.O.P. Eugster, DSO, OBE, MC, Irish Guards. The regimental sergeant major was RSM D.T. Lynch, DCM, Irish Guards. Stand these two men on top of one another and they would have reached the top of the Tower. Colonel Eugster was a big man, but RSM Lynch was a giant. He was over six feet four inches high and he combined this height with an enormous girth. If we had stood these two on top of one another, the RSM would have been the man on the ground floor and the colonel would have been on the first floor.

The RSM was probably the most celebrated sergeant major then serving in the British Army and this was in the days when sergeant majors were national celebrities. Perhaps the most famous of all was RSM Brittain. So famous did he become during his time that he was able to retire from the Army and pursue a very successful career on stage and television. He was the great stereotype sergeant major and he even appeared in a Royal Variety Performance. He made commercials and radio programmes, but his finest hour was an appearance on Top of the Pops.

RSM Brittain was followed by J.C. Lord. Lord was the RSM at Sandhurst and welcomed all new officer cadets with his famous self-introduction.

'My name,' pause, 'is Regimental Sergeant Major J.C.Lord,' pause, 'JC doesn't stand for Jesus Christ,' pause. 'He is the Lord above and I am the lord down here!'

Then, in our time, there was RSM Lynch. His huge stature combined with a voice like an Irish Pavarotti made his parade ground manner famous throughout the British Army. Furthermore, he was probably impersonated by more people than was Norman Wisdom. Within a week or two we could all do a passable impersonation of the RSM. Whenever two or three officer cadets from Eaton Hall were gathered together in their off-duty time, they would soon be transformed into the RSM, such that the good people of Chester soon became accustomed to whole platoons of RSM Lynchs marching up and down the public streets issuing a series of commands in an incomprehensible Irish brogue. It reminds me of some of the mass gatherings of Elvis lookalikes who hold great conventions around the world.

As well as the RSM from the Irish Guards, there were several other famous Guards sergeant majors at Eaton Hall. Each of the four companies had its own company sergeant major, each from a different branch of the Brigade. A Coy was under the direction of CSM Blood of the Coldstream Guards. B Coy came under CSM 'Barney' Owen of the Grenadier Guards and C Coy responded (pretty sharply) to CSM Leach of the Scots Guards. Paddy Rafter of the Irish Guards was the sergeant major with D Coy. Lynch, Blood and Leach were a fine trio to serve as an introduction to Eaton Hall. The names alone struck terror into the hearts and minds of us poor young cadets.

These were men at the very pinnacle of their profession, probably the finest sergeant majors then serving in the British Army; formidable, fantastic men. If marching and parade ground skills had been Olympic events, these guys would have been standing shoulder to shoulder on the rostrum collecting the medals. And how they would stand! What posture, what style! Anyone who has never seen a Guards sergeant major on parade can never really understand the meaning of the word 'smart'.

Our company sergeant major was Sergeant Major Blood of the Coldstream Guards. He was a Yorkshireman and he brought to the Army all the qualities of efficiency, reliability and loyalty that are associated with men from that county. He wasn't as tall as most Warrant Officers in the Guards, but he made up for it by sheer class. Both on the parade ground and off it, he was a consummate soldier, the absolute professional. From his Coldstream white peaked hat through his scarlet sash, down to his boots, shining like black diamonds, he was the very picture of military breeding. He terrified us. He cursed and cajoled us. He harried and hounded us. During the next four months we would be moulded by CSM Blood. Every day for four months we were at his mercy. During those four months all of us passed through the full range of emotion about CSM Blood, from abject fear, to grudging respect, to admiration and finally overwhelming affection. In every walk of life there are people who are so good at what they do that the mere thought of them in action brings a little shudder of appreciation down the spine. CSM Blood was the best. He took a bunch of nineteen-year-old officer cadets and he showed them by example how to conduct themselves in the world in which they found themselves.

On the very first day, our relationship with our training NCOs was beautifully explained to us by Blood. He addressed us on the parade ground, where he gave us most of his insights. He would, he said, be addressing each of us as 'sir' reflecting our new status as provisional officers. On the other hand we would also be addressing *him* as 'sir'. It would be a mistake, he added, if we were to interpret this as an exchange between equals. When he addressed us as 'sir' he would be observing the Army manual; when we called him 'sir', we would bloody well mean it!

We still served in our respective regiments. For instance Jumbo, Grandad Farrar, Tony Swinson, the Mole and I were still in the Buffs. We still wore the shoulder flashes, cap badge and insignia of the Buffs. All the others also wore the little distinguishing marks of their regiments. Scotsmen wore kilts, the Marines wore their distinctive peaked hats and white belts, the Rifle Brigade wore their black buttons and green berets. In fact the only markings that we all had in common were little white gorgets with buttons on them, which we wore on the lapels of our battledress to signify that we were learner officers.

We might easily have looked more like Vaudeville than a company of officer cadets had not CSM Blood been able to make us march like one man. Different regiments, different headgear, some in skirts, and yet Blood was able to produce precision and togetherness such as I have never experienced anywhere else in my life.

12

DAMN FINE PIGEON

Eaton Hall was not run only by non-commissioned offic-ers. The campus was swarming with awficers as well. In the late 1950s the Regular Army offered a much more permanent career to professional officers than it does today. Officers who were energetically seeking promotion eagerly sought a posting on the staff at Eaton Hall. Because a spell at Eaton Hall looked good on the military equivalent of a CV, many of the brightest and the best in the British Army turned up here. Some of them were guardsmen. Not only the commanding officer, but also the adjutant and the assistant adjutant were traditionally seconded from the Brigade of Guards. But the other officers were drawn from all the different infantry regi-ments of the British Army.

Each platoon of cadets had a platoon commander who carried the rank of captain. Each company consisted of only two platoons and was commanded by a major; so the teacher/pupil ratio was fairly powerful. My platoon commander was called Captain Freeman-Wallace of the Hampshire Regiment. Double-barrelled names were de rigeur in the officer class, but we decided to improve his prospects even more by adding an extra hyphen. We soon decided that he should in fact be treble-barrelled to improve his chances of promotion and so he was always referred to as Captain Freeman-Hardy-Willis after the shoe store. He was much involved in our training on a day-to-day basis and, in addition, he was the new carrier of the Army's most potent weapon, the clipboard. He now was the one who followed us everywhere taking notes of every little detail about us. Our future was in his hands, because his report would form the basis for decisions on whether we were suitable to complete the course and become officers. Furthermore, even if we did get through the course, there was still another hurdle to be overcome. By now most of us had some idea which regiment we would like to be commissioned into. But it was by no means certain that our chosen regiment would accept us. This would be decided on all sorts of factors. Some chaps' fathers had served in the regiment of their choice. Depending on the success or otherwise of their dads, this was normally an advantage. Other chaps had good connections with the current senior officers serving in the regiment to which they would apply. There was a lot of,

'Young Johnny's boy! You know Johnny Bartholomew. Chap who comes hunting with us. Bought you a drink at the polo. You remember. Splendid chap. Well his lad wants to join us. Think we should have him what, what!'

But for those of us whose fathers had been Air Raid Wardens in the war, or who thought polo was a mint with a hole, there was a certain amount of peeping at the platoon commander's confidential report.

The East Surrey Regiment was not noted for its aristocratic connections, but it was noted for something else for which I had no form at all. The East Surrey Regiment was famed throughout the Army for its prowess at sports. The first battalion of the East Surrey Regiment, which was the unit to which we national service officers would be posted if we were accepted, was currently stationed in Brunswick in Germany.

The commanding officer was Lt Colonel Clive Wallis, who had played rugby for Ireland before the war. Because of his ferocious commitment to sport of every kind, the East Surreys were BAOR (British Army of the Rhine) champions at rugby, athletics, hockey, cricket, boxing and probably would have been champions at ping-pong if Colonel Clive had thought that it was a proper Man's game.

While some regiments looked out for chaps with double-barrelled names and a receding jaw line, the East Surreys were on the lookout for sportsmen. It was no surprise that their fifth column had already made approaches to the Mole. By this time the Mole had become my best pal and I had decided that I would like to try to go with him into the East Surreys. This clearly required some fairly heavy crawling. The Mole himself was not averse to trying to help me, but I think, with the benefit of hindsight, his insistence that he would like to bring 'a friend' probably raised a few eyebrows at HQ and did not do much to advance my cause. Basically, I just had to fall back on my ability to impress Captain Freeman-Hardy-Willis.

Most of us were in the same boat. Every time the captain appeared, the whole platoon would leap into overdrive to make sure he did not jot down anything adverse on his bloody little clipboard. Failure to be accepted into the regiment of your choice was almost the same as failing the Wozzer. Those who were rejected were assigned arbitrarily by the War Office to make up the numbers in regiments from some of the more obscure counties.

Since our captain was following our progress on a day-to-day basis, it was anticipated that he would have a fairly deep insight into our character, which would form the basis of his reports on us. After about ten weeks of training and intensive study by the platoon commander, he had a one-on-one session with each of us in turn.

When my turn came, I was in a state of high anxiety

because, by now, it had become pretty clear that the competition to join the Surreys was becoming particularly severe and all would depend on Freeman-Hardy-Willis's evaluation.

He sat at a desk in the company commander's office. He had acknowledged my sharp knock on the door with a very languid 'Come'. I strode in and slammed to a shuddering halt in front of him and let fly with a salute from Heaven.

'Do sit down,' he said in his most patronising voice, as he pulled out the personal file that had been resting at his elbow. Slowly he opened it and seemed to peruse the contents in silence for a long time.

'Well, now, Hudson. We are not really pleased in every department,' he drawled.

'Thorne, sir. I'm Thorne, sir,' I blurted.

'Oh are you?' he sighed. 'Well just stop going around looking like Hudson will you,' he barked at me.

'Sir. Right, sir.'

It was fairly apparent that my efforts to impress the platoon commander had not been an unqualified success. However, in spite of the setback, I persevered in the hope that something favourable might slip on to his clipboard. And yet there was another member of the platoon who tried even harder to catch the eye of the captain. Unfortunately the more Larry Shore tried to impress, the more prone he was to disaster. Much of his time on the parade ground was spent in a sort of single file, owing to his slightly eccentric sense of direction; so he just knew he had to develop other skills in his military repertoire if he was to make it through to graduation.

Captain Freeman-Hardy marched us out to the weapon training area and, unfortunately, Larry saw this as one of those opportunities to catch the eye.

We were scheduled to bone up our skills at firing anti-tank rockets and throwing hand grenades. We were dressed in full battle kit, which included tin hats, great packs on our backs and pouches pressing up on our chests like loaded brassieres. We marched out to the weapon training area, which lay quite deep in the grounds of the ancient pile at what was clearly considered to be a safe distance from the old monstrosity. It went unremarked that a small medical orderly seemed to have attached himself to our platoon for this morning's particular exercise.

The weapon training area was not the range, which we had visited on several occasions to practise with our old Lee Enfields; this was an area of about fifty square yards totally enclosed by barbed wire. All around were huge signs featuring a grinning skull, which ominously bore a striking resemblance to Larry Shore, with an exclamation mark, together with great notices shrieking 'DANGER' or 'HIGH EXPLOSIVES'. At the far end of the range was an old rusting tank, which was to simulate the target. And at the near end of the area was a sort of concrete pillbox, which was immediately alongside a dug-out trench, which was the throwing area for grenade throwers. The whole distance from the firing area to the tank was only about twenty-five yards.

The warriors of No. 1 Platoon assembled in the little dug-out area to receive instruction from our captain. The two-man anti-tank rocket-launcher was to be the first toy we would play with. One man lay down just forward of the trench with a thing like a piece of old drainpipe wrapped around his shoulders. It was the job of the other member of the team to stuff a rocket about the size of a large marrow up the back. Then the reclining chap would point the whole contraption in the direction of the tank and pull the trigger. A sheet of flame scorched down the back of the poor bloke lying down, while the rocket loader hopped around fairly lively in the rear.

Out of ten firing squads, only two managed to hit the tank, even though it was well within the distance that an average thrower might throw the rocket and be fairly confident of hitting the target. This lack of accuracy probably had something to do with the anticipation of the huge roaring explosion that was accompanied by a ten foot sheet of flame that hurtled out of the back of the bazooka. Since the man lying down, trying to aim the wretched thing, bore the brunt of this, it was not surprising that most of us had a slight tendency to flinch at the *moment critique*.

Those that did strike the target were rewarded with a loud clanging sound as metal struck metal. Fortunately, the rockets were not armed. It was fairly clear to all of us that, had they been, the subsequent explosion would have done about equal damage to the occupants of the tank and to the few members of the firing squad who had survived the actual firing of the weapon.

Captain made it pretty clear that he was not satisfied with our success rate with the bazooka and berated the platoon for a marked lack of fortitude in the aim. Bertie Bois mentioned that perhaps we would stand a better chance of hitting the target if El Capitano gave us a personal demonstration, but he was too clever to fall for that one, pointing out that ammunition was in short supply and was not to be wasted on accomplished operators.

For his pains Bertie was immediately teamed with Larry Shore as the next two-man team. Larry was designated as the lying-down man and Bertie was the 'Light-the-blue-touch-paper-and-run man'. The captain gave strict instructions that the firer was not to flinch but was to maintain his aim throughout the operation.

Bertie did a pretty nimble job around the back and Larry held deadly straight waiting for the command, 'Fire!'

Unfortunately, Larry was a fairly little bloke and he was not all that well anchored to the ground. As he pulled the trigger there was an enormous explosion and a streak of flame leapt from the back of the rocket launcher. Larry shot forward towards the target, while his rocket lobbed harmlessly towards square leg, missing the tank by at least twenty yards.

Freeman-Hardy-Willis made it pretty clear that he was about as unimpressed with Larry's performance in weapon training as on the parade ground and we all sensed, with a certain amount of foreboding, that Larry was determined to make up for this with a particularly strong effort in the grenade throwing.

Unlike the bazooka rockets, the grenades we were to play with were the real thing in every way. They had the familiar acorn shape made of indented gunmetal. They were packed with explosive and designed to spread a swathe of deadly shrapnel over an area the size of a cricket pitch. There was a two-inch spring clip that was held in place by the sort of split pin technology used in old-fashioned lavatory cisterns. Once the pin has been removed, only your hand clasped around the spring clip stands between you and a big bang.

The captain explained the ground rules. We would take turns to stand alongside him in the dugout. On his instructions we would remove the firing pin and then, on the count of three, we should try to throw the grenade as far as possible. Any officer cadet worth his salt should easily be able to throw the grenade clean out of the compound. 'Remember, Pin Out and Throw the Grenade! Not the Other Way Round!' 'Ha,ha,ha!'

We had all seen these grenades in the movies, but they turned out to be a lot heavier than we imagined. John Wayne threw them about one hundred and fifty yards right on to the head of a fleeing Jappo. Larry Shore didn't.

None of us had much success getting great distance on the throw. It was awkward to be encumbered by all the paraphernalia of the full battle kit. Jumbo Fuller was about the longest. Using the same technique that he employed in the outfield, he got some length on his throw, but, even he was well inside the compound and was only greeted with a rather grudging 'Not bad', from the captain. Most of us were a lot shorter than that. I had experienced some difficulty getting my throwing arm over the trench and my grenade had exploded perilously close to the lip of our little dugout.

'Who's f . . . ing side are you on, Hudson?' said the captain as we both dived for cover.

But for Larry this was his big chance to get something right. He marched into the dugout alongside Freeman-Hardy. His teeth were gritted and his fists clenched as he pumped the adrenalin through his system. He was going to be the one who hit the jackpot. His grenade was going to soar out of the compound. 'Get your clipboard ready, Freeman-Hardy. Just get a load of this!'

Inevitably, Larry was left-handed. But here he was at Iwo Jima. He wound himself up like an Olympic discus thrower from the Eastern Bloc. Silence descended on the watching comrades. As the captain said, 'Throw!' he nonchalantly pulled the pin from his grenade and then, quite suddenly, started to rotate like a whirling dervish. As he spun on his axis, his tin hat fell forward over his eyes and, with a curious corkscrew action he launched his mighty throw.

There was no question Larry had the distance, but there did seem to be a problem developing on the direction. Larry's grenade shot straight upwards, immediately above the dugout. The captain stood momentarily transfixed. It soon became clear to the rest of us that Larry's grenade was heading straight back whence it came. There was a sudden outburst of frenzied activity as we all headed for the safety of the little concrete pillbox.

'Aw my Gawd,' drawled Freeman-Hardy as slowly the awful truth dawned on him. Then all dignity departed as panic struck. He covered the fifteen feet from the exposure of the throwing zone to the safety of the pillbox in less time than it took the rest of us to turn and pray. He arrived in a heap of flailing arms and legs, a far cry from the smooth, stiff upper-lipped captain that we had learned to love. All triple barrels of the captain collapsed in a heap at our feet. Freeman was piled on top of Hardy, with Willis smeared all over the floor.

Meanwhile, Larry stood in splendid isolation in the middle of the throwing area, struggling with the headband of his tin hat and wondering why the lights had gone out. His grenade seemed to hang in the air for an eternity. Slowly, it stopped going up and started coming down. It looked like a certain direct hit. Larry slowly pushed his hat back on to the top of his dome-shaped head and started peering into the distance over on the far side of the compound where he was confidently expecting to see his grenade take out at least two dozen Japanese. The grenade descended gently from immediately overhead, caught a glancing blow on the very rim of Larry's tin hat and then did an 'in-off' over the front of the dugout. A huge chorus of 'Get down you stupid arse . . .' was interrupted by a blinding flash and an ear-ripping crash. The enormous pressure of the blast drove Larry downwards where he practically corkscrewed through the bottom of the trench. His little charred corpse lay motionless.

'Nice one, eh,' he said.

The company commander was called Major Vivian Earle. He came from the South Lancashire Regiment. He was a pretty stylish chap for such an unfashionable regiment. Somehow, he would have looked more at home in the Rifle Brigade where many of the famous old families made up the officers' mess. I suspect that his family had probably served in the South Lancs for generations. He, himself, was certainly of the old school, charming, elegant and distinctly upper class.

This elegant and nice man had much less contact with us than our platoon commander and yet he always knew my name and seemed to be generally interested in all the cadets in his company. Unfortunately, my only real contact with the company commander was when I came before him on a charge.

This was all a clear case of mistaken identity and it involved another of the officers at Eaton Hall who deserves a mention, namely the assistant adjutant.

The adjutant and his assistant were part of the folklore. They were both stunningly beautiful as behoves men in their position, because their main role was, of course, to ponce about on the parade ground. They were both from the Brigade of Guards which meant that they would spend a lot of their parade time peering out from under those huge bearskin hats which guardsmen wear and which give them such an air of superiority. The principal quality demanded of a good adjutant is a monstrous parade ground affectation, a sort of prettiness on parade. These boys were at the very pinnacle of their trade.

Eaton Hall's adjutant was Captain Mayfield of the Scots Guards. He was, of course, re-named Captain Mayfly. He was just like a toy soldier and, on parade, he was all flutter and finesse with beautiful vowels which contrasted magnificently with the Irish brogue of the RSM.

But the real megastar was the assistant adjutant, who was called Captain Peter Egerton-Warburton. Actually it is possible that he was only a lieutenant, but he certainly was an acting captain and he had all the style and arrogance of a Four Star General. He was tall, blonde and blazingly good-looking in an aristocratic way. He looked as though he had just stepped off the stage from some restoration comedy. His sword flashed in the sunlight and his bearskin sat halfway down his face. But his real speciality was equestrian. He frequently took the morning adjutant's parade, while the Mayfly saved himself for the really big occasions, and he loved to make the grand entrance mounted on a white charger. As soon as Egerton-Warburton appeared on parade he was the focus of all attention. Even the vast figure of the regimental sergeant major could not compete with shining leather thigh boots, silver spurs and a horse. What is more, the assistant adjutant could make flamboyant and wafty gestures from on top of his horse, which would have marked him out in the corps de ballet.

In an earlier edition of this book Peter Egerton-Warburton was referred to as 'a sort of effeminate Peter O'Toole'. However, I am pleased to acknowledge that this description may have given a false impression of his inclinations. In order to prevent an outbreak of a false sense of security among the female population of Hampshire, I am happy to put the record straight. At the time of our attendance at Eaton Hall, Peter Warburton was just twenty-four years old and he had already incurred the wrath of the hierarchy of the Coldstream Guards by marrying a film starlet when he was only twenty years old.

Furthermore he continued this practice of marrying beautiful women at fairly regular intervals during the rest of his life, which I am pleased to record, is still continuing. And, finally, if there should ever be any further doubt on this issue I could relate the story of some frontline activities in Tangier which resulted in quite serious injuries that have acquired cult status in the medical history of his regiment. However, since he also acquired a further reputation as a boxer (he boxed for the Army), I am inclined to move on.

It was Egerton-Warburton who was to be my downfall. Sometimes on the adjutant's morning parade the whole college would line up stretched across the parade ground in single file. This was to provide a backdrop for the platoon, which was passing out. Whenever we were practising for one of the platoons senior to us, we would fall in in this formation. Every position was pre-assigned to create exactly the right effect. We would form a giant pyramid. The tallest cadet would take up position on a marked spot right in the centre. Then everyone would line up on either side of him in order of height so that the column would slope gently downwards to either side, towards the two smallest men in the college who would form the right and left marker respectively.

The early morning sun was eclipsed as the huge figure of RSM Lynch marched on to the parade ground. With the marvellous emphasis on all the consonants that is the character of the Irish,

'Tallest in Te Middle. Smallest Atteech End,' pause, 'Fallin!'

After less than a few seconds of swarming, the whole parade would be re-formed, perfectly spaced, motionless. One magnificent single file of mathematical precision lined across the parade ground ready for the passing-out platoon to march out behind the band. Immediately behind the long file stood the drill sergeants and the four company sergeant majors ready to pounce on the slightest quiver.

Before the passing-out platoon marched on to the square, the whole parade would be pre-empted by the spectacular arrival of the Queen of Hearts herself. Mounted on his regular white horse, the assistant adjutant made his daring entrance. His saddlery, his sword and his spurs all glinted in the morning sun. The huge RSM marched towards him, like a tank approaching the cavalry. I could feel the asphalt shudder beneath my feet as the RSM slammed his huge boots downwards as he made his halt. Even though the assistant adjutant was mounted, the RSM seemed to be on a level with where his eyes might have been, had they not been hidden inside the bearskin. The RSM's salute was the prototype for every sergeant major in the British Army.

'Carry on Saarnt Mayjaw!' wailed the little beauty.

The RSM did an about turn that swivelled in one perfect movement and, again, the earth moved as his huge boots slammed downwards.

Just as the RSM was about to give the command to march the passing-out platoon on to the square, Egerton-Warburton intervened.

'Saarnt Mayjaw, thar is a man thar moving on parade. Little man on the end thar!'

The assistant adjutant could see nothing from under his

bearskin, but he made an airy-fairy arm gesture waving his unsheathed sword in the direction of the little man at the right hand end of the long column. I was the left marker at the opposite end of the line so I was particularly dismayed when CSM Blood, who was parading immediately behind me, jerked his sergeant major's stick into the small of my back and cried out to the whole parade,

'I've Gottim, sir. Officer Cadet Thorne, sir. Moving on Parade, sir!'

This was a chargeable offence and I was duly summoned to appear on Company Commander's Orders. On the day my case came up, I paraded in the sergeant major's office and was ordered to remove my beret and my belt. Feeling almost naked, I was marched across to the company command-er's office by CSM Blood, where we waited outside. As I stood to attention, the CSM lined up about one millime-tre behind me breathing down my neck. At the company commander's instruction I was marched forward a few paces in double time.

'LeftRightLeftRightAlt!'

I stood to attention like a petrified rock while Sgt Major Blood read out the charge.

Major Earle was benign. He looked up at me from behind his desk like a kindly uncle expressing concern and disap-pointment at my fall from grace.

'Ah, Thorne. This is the first time we have had you on a charge. You have heard what the sergeant major has said. This is quite serious, moving on the adjutant's parade. Now, do you have anything to say?'

I felt the sergeant major's hot breath on my collar and I heard a pathetic little voice speaking all in a rush.

'I think the sergeant major got the wrong man, sir.'

'The wrong man! What do you mean the wrong man?' said Major Earle in a most solicitous voice.

'Well, sir, the adjutant pointed to a little man moving on

parade, sir. He pointed to the right, sir and I was the left marker, sir.'

'Case dismissed,' said the major somewhat airily.

A gruff Yorkshire voice from behind me snapped out 'About Turn!'

I turned about and my nose pressed up against CSM Blood's great chest. He took one great stride to his left placing himself alongside me.

'Officer Cadet Thorne. At the double, Queeck Mar!'

I shot out of the company commander's office like a cork out of a bottle. Blood double-marched me some fifty yards in nine point eight seconds.

'And Don't Tell Me I Can't See Which Way a Sword is Pointing, You Half-Cocked, Sawn-Off Little . . .'

Major Earle also gave us a series of lectures on all aspects of officerliness. He was a lively and interesting speaker, but sometimes the lectures were timed mid-way through an afternoon, following a morning of outdoor warfare. On those occasions another enemy would sometimes stalk the lecture room. An awful drowsiness would overcome some of the aspiring officers.

On one occasion the major was giving a lecture to the whole company about the interaction of the Army with the Civil Defence Forces in the aftermath of a nuclear war. While this was an important subject which we needed to master, we all knew that the sort of nuclear war that then threatened would be very unlikely to leave much of a Civil Defence, or much of an Army, to interact. In a way the whole subject was a bit hypothetical. But, in addition, it was about 3.30 in the afternoon of a very cold day in March. We had paraded at 7.30 that morning and had then been out on manoeuvres, viciously attacking C Coy all over the training area. Now the sun was going down in our eyes and the lecture room was overheated by a coal fire in the middle of the room.

Bertie Bois was sitting in the front row on my right. John Farrar was sitting on his other side. I saw Bertie's eyes rolling skywards several times. Each time I saw him shake his head and peer forward again at the major as though hanging on his every word. But finally his eyes seemed to disappear behind his eyelids as his head sank forward on to his hands, which were clasped in front of him. In the Great Battle of Nod, Bertie had run up the white flag.

Major Earle was describing the reporting structure in the Civil Defence Force when Bertie started to snore very quietly in the front row.

'So,' said the major, 'what then is the codename for a district commander in the Civil Defence?'

He looked slowly around the assembly selecting the cadet who would be given the chance to score a point by answering this easy question.

'Officer Cadet Bois.'

John Farrar gave Bertie the most imperceptible nudge with his left elbow and Bertie's head slipped off its resting place on his hands on to the wooden desk beneath with a slight thump.

'Oh,' he said, startled to see the major immediately in front of him pointing a little lecture stick at him.

'I agree with the last speaker, sir.'

'No one has spoken yet, Bois,' said the major.

Bertie re-engaged the grey cells with a speed that did credit to his chances of becoming an officer.

'Then I agree with the next speaker, sir.'

Major Earle's most worthy lecture was on 'Man Management'. The purpose of this particular lecture was to give potential officers some insight into the psychology of leadership. He taught us how to conduct ourselves towards the men in our charge in order to gain their trust and support. He described the sort of incongruous group of men we might be expected to find in the average infantry platoon and gave us his tips on how to deal with them. He covered the whole spectrum from the traditional 'Hard Case' to the lonely outsider. Needless to say, he was at his most sympathetic when dealing with the latter category. He described how he had taken command of a platoon of the South Lancs when he himself had just been commissioned second lieutenant from Sandhurst.

His platoon mainly consisted of Lancastrian tattoo merchants. But, one young soldier who seemed to be the classic loner, unable to take part in any of the social activities of the platoon troubled him. Apparently, this man was called Martin and the major described how he had gone out of his way to find out what particular interests Martin had.

Eventually, he was able to find out from one of his corporals that Martin had a great interest in ornithology. So the major, or second lieutenant-cum-psychiatrist as he was then, sought an opportunity to talk to Martin on his favourite subject.

The opportunity arose when they were watching a platoon football match. Martin was also a spectator, but, as usual, he was standing on his own about fifteen yards away from the rest of the group.

Suddenly, a large bird landed right in the middle of the pitch and the major seized his chance. He drew on all his reserves of Man Management and strode over to Martin,

'I say! Damn Fine Pigeon.'

13

IN POSITION

We passed out from Eaton Hall on 17 May 1957. The sense of achievement was colossal. I learned the week before that I had been accepted to serve as a second lieutenant with the East Surrey Regiment.

The only possible blemish on my excursion to Heaven was that the time had come to say goodbye to some colleagues with whom I had become closer than any group of people before or since. The key to forming real friendship is exposure to a common enemy. In a way, throughout our training, the Army had been that enemy and, in our common fear of the unknown and unexpected, we had all come to a form of intimacy that was unique. The only place I can imagine where greater friendships might be formed would be somewhere like Wormwood Scrubs.

Jumbo Fuller and old Grandad Farrar joined the Queen's Regiment, the West Surreys. It was an irony that, towards the very end of our service, plans would be afoot to merge the Queen's Regiment and the East Surrey Regiment. In fact we never did rejoin our old mates in the Queen's, because an emergency in the Middle East saw the Surreys off into action.

The whole merger had to be delayed until just after we were demobbed. But I would meet up with Jumbo again when he shot down Jesus Lane, Cambridge, on a rusty old bike.

'What Ho, Captain!' he yelled across the street at me, 'I'm looking for my tutor in a virgin's asshole.'

It turned out that his tutor kept rooms in 'The Maid's Causeway', which was one of the ancient streets running close to Jesus Lane.

Old Grandad went back to the two loves of his life and prospered with both. He finally won the fourth round of his long-running bout with the examiners from the Royal Institution of Chartered Surveyors and he married Shirley who was the great love of his life.

Bertie Bois had successfully defied the system. He must have been the only person to have been chucked out of Sandhurst and then earn a commission as a national serviceman. He stayed with the Buffs.

Dear Tony Swinson, Christian and upright, but still with a beret that looked like a cowpat, joined the Yorks and Lancs Regiment, where he could, at last, chuck away his beret and doff the peaked cap of an officer.

Dear old Webby was in the squad behind us so he had to soldier on for a while before he, too, passed out along with David Ford who was to join the East Surrey Regiment. I mention David here because he played a continuing part in this dramatic story, while the others went their separate ways. John Webb went off to Nigeria with the West African Rifles where a fellow-officer was Jack Gowan who played such a prominent part in that country's history during and after the Biafran war. But Webby survived to share a room with me at Jesus College, Cambridge.

Butch Mackenzie Hill joined the Marines where his flying fists continued to earn him an interesting reputation, which he was later able to enlarge at Cambridge. His career at that establishment was nearly ended before it began as a result of a slightly exuberant reunion party in the opening days of the first term. Butch Hill's new landlady was a bit unsympathetic towards her new lodger when he returned after the party and she called the proctor to attend to him. The proctor is a part of the university establishment who is a sort of one man Flying Squad and is responsible for discipline amongst the undergraduate community. He has two particularly fearsome assistants, called 'bulldogs', who do much of the physical bit. This was the little team that assembled outside Mr Mackenzie Hill's room, which happened to be on the first floor.

The proctor has a certain old-world charm in the manner in which he addresses even the most spirited member of the university. He raised his black mortar board in greeting and declared in a loud voice that he required to address himself to Mr Mackenzie Hill.

Suddenly, the upper window burst open and the sought-after undergraduate appeared quite naked and relieved himself prodigiously on the ancient authorities below.

Apparently, it is rare for a member of the university to be sent down so early in his career, so the College authorities put the whole matter down to an oversight on Butch's part; he was allowed to stay on, to the great advantage of the boxing team.

Larry Shore survived the course in spite of a few hitches along the way. He was commissioned into the Glosters. Apparently his confidential report recommended that his new unit allow him to develop his career in a desk-bound capacity. He too arrived at Cambridge after his service had ended. He proved himself to be a brilliant engineer.

Meanwhile, amongst the fond farewells that followed graduation from Eaton Hall, I had to say goodbye to another old friend.

Officers have different Army numbers and I was no longer 23339788. The new number was quite insignificant and I now have no recollection of it. By contrast, 23339788 will stick with me all my days.

And the Mole and I moved on to join the East Surrey Regiment. We had two weeks' leave after which we were to report to the regimental depot at Kingston. There we waited to be despatched to Germany where we would join the first battalion.

Mole's leave was interrupted by a full-scale emergency. The East Surreys had reached the finals of the BAOR athletics championships and one of the regiment's sprint relay team had pulled a hamstring. Mole was airlifted to the frontline and thrown straight into the sort of action that was to keep him busy for most of the rest of his service. The demand for my services was less pressing, so I had to report alone to the regimental depot.

The depot was a backwater. It acted as a staging post for East Surrey personnel who were in transit from the first battalion to other destinations. While the 'real' East Surreys were in Brunswick, officers and men were frequently moving back and forth between Germany and some other department of the Army where they might be attending a course or on some other assignment. Officers were always being posted between the first battalion and the War Office or the Staff College at Camberley. The regimental depot was a sort of dropping off point for all these itinerants and all this transience generated a very lackadaisical atmosphere. There were always a few invalids hobbling around. The regimental band was there, 'resting between engagements', when I reported, together with quite a few odds and sods who were just hanging about.

Amongst the odds and sods were ex-Cpl Bean and Pte Fulford. Both of these two gentlemen had been serving with the regiment in Brunswick when they had separately remembered pressing engagements back home in Blighty. Cpl Bean had received reports of a little local action involving his wife

who was apparently celebrating his absence a little osten-
tatiously, while Pte Fulford had beaten up a traffic policeman in Brunswick and had decided that his best defence was
absence. The military police had picked up both deserters
and had returned them to the regimental depot. A court
martial had been convened to hear their cases in Brunswick
and they were just waiting for an officer to escort them back
to Germany.

The friendly adjutant at the depot explained to me how
anxious these two men were to rejoin the battalion. I would
have no trouble at all, he said, so long as I kept the two of
them handcuffed together and never let them out of my sight
during the whole journey. Furthermore, he explained how
lucky I was because they had assigned L/Cpl Remnant to
complete the escort party.

Only later did I discover that Brian Remnant was a
national serviceman who was younger than I was. He was
no more a lance corporal than a hole in the ground and
the crafty devils at the depot had promoted him as acting,
unpaid lance corporal for the duration of the journey only,
so that they could get rid of him. He had been sent back
home from the first battalion for further medical tests after
he had developed what was loosely described by the MO
in Brunswick as 'Nervous Unsettlement'. In spite of the
fact that he was clearly barking mad, the medical boys back
home had decided that he was just 'skiving' and he should
be returned to active duty. He was to cause me much more
grief than either of the two prisoners.

One old major, who seemed to have come to rest permanently at the depot, gave me great encouragement. He told
me the story of a former second lieutenant, called Barry
Aldridge, who had also been despatched from Kingston to
join the battalion with an important consignment. This was a
pair of valuable regimental pistols, which had been returned
for repairs to the armourer who worked at the depot. It was

Aldridge's job to take this precious cargo back to Brunswick. The pistols were boxed up in a small wooden case no bigger than a hatbox. Just as to me, the friendly adjutant at the depot had said,

'Don't let them out of your sight on the journey, my boy.'

Aldridge stayed locked to his little box. Once he had safely embarked on the troop ship to cross the Channel, he had ventured into the officers' bar on board and had stood at the bar with one foot planted firmly on the precious cargo. Then, later, he was gently resting in his bunk when he heard the ship's public address system bark out,

'Would the officer of the East Surrey Regiment who left the regimental pistols in the bar kindly report to the purser's office to collect them.'

By the time I reached the bar on my troop ship, I felt I deserved a drink. The journey from Kingston to Harwich had been made exclusively on public transport, starting with a bus ride from outside the depot to the railway station at Kingston.

Fortunately, I was spared the embarrassment of asking the conductor for,

'One, and two convicts to the station, please,' because the Army had at least given me some vouchers to pay for the trip.

In the train from Liverpool Street to Harwich Brian Remnant had developed catastrophic hiccups. Probably this is a well-known symptom of 'Nervous Unsettlement', but it served to draw even more attention to the incongruous little party in uniform and it became very apparent that the members of the public on the train were trying to move further and further away from us. I was considerably more relieved to hand Remnant over to the field hospital on the ship than I was to see Bean and Fulford locked away in the ship's clink.

Finally, I made it into the ship's bar where I was able to forget for a moment the daunting prospect of dragging this circus half way across Europe from the Hook of Holland to

Brunswick in the far north east of Germany. Then I heard a voice on the public address system repeating the Aldridge nightmare.

'Would the officer in charge of the contingent from the East Surrey Regiment report at once to the purser's office.'

My heart sank as I speculated whether the deserters or Remnant had run amok.

In the purser's office I was met by a sergeant in the military police. He was holding a bedraggled and frightened young soldier. I could see at a glance that he was not one of my party, but, equally, I could see that he was wearing the unmistakable insignia of the East Surreys.

'Deserter, sir,' said the sergeant, 'picked him up ashore, sir. You are to take him back with you to the battalion, sir, where he is wanted on a serious charge, sir.'

'What's the charge?' I said, despairingly.

'Murder, sir.'

Brunswick, or Braunschweig as the Germans called it, was a fine city about fifty miles to the east of Hanover. The city itself had suffered a few scars from the war, but that did not prevent us from appreciating a handsome and ancient regional capital. But the real significance of Brunswick was that it lay almost directly on the border between East and West. The Russians manned their side of the border and we had an observation post, which had to be manned by a posse of East Surreys around the clock, at a place called Helmstedt. There were two border points within a couple of miles of the barracks at Brunswick. One was Helmstedt and the other was Wolfburg just a fraction to the north. In the Cold War, we were on the absolute frontline.

The barracks themselves had been custom-built for some of the Führer's crack Panzer troops and they constituted almost a city within the city. All British service quarters have a distinctly utilitarian look. But this was not the style of our recent opponents. We had a camp cinema the size of the Odeon, Leicester Square, an indoor sports complex that included a full-size hockey pitch and an officers' mess like the Taj Mahal. There was a gymnasium that could have been a venue for the Olympic Games, swimming pools and acres of playing fields. The East Surrey Regiment was in its element.

We were a little community inside the city of Brunswick, totally self-contained. There were married quarters that stretched for miles; there was a church and shops and bus services, all within the military compound.

These palatial premises were occupied by one full-strength fighting battalion, which consisted of about a thousand persons. There were wives and children, with their own school. These occupied the married quarters, which the Germans had very thoughtfully provided. These were all skilfully graded from the CO's house, which was a tastefully presented mansion, to several dozen small villas for the wives and families of the corporals and even some lance corporals.

We were about the size of a mid-sized English village, all going about our business just two miles away from the Bad Guys, who were massed on the other side of the border. Here we all were with our doctors and dentists, teachers and chaplains, postmen and flower arrangers, defending the Free World. We were 'In Position'.

The military activity, such that it was, was very different from Eaton Hall. Here were no Guards adjutants on mounted chargers. Our adjutants were deskbound chaps who undid their jackets on a hot day and wrestled with the paperwork demanded by the day to day task of trying to keep a whole battalion occupied.

We had an RSM, but he was a far cry from RSM Lynch. His name was RSM Oram and he was known to all and sundry as 'Peachey' Oram. Most of the sergeants called him Peachey to his face and even the colonel called him Peachey.

This was a fair comment on his sunny complexion, which he had developed in the course of his duties. Because here, in the real world of active service, the most important job for the RSM was to be an outstanding host in the sergeants' mess and, as I was to learn, there was no more genial host than Peachey. His other duties would include organising the children's sports day and decorating the whole barracks at Christmas time.

About a half of the total number of private soldiers and junior NCOs were national servicemen. Keeping them occupied was not too much of a challenge because they all maintained their dedication to their 'gloat charts'. Hours could be spent refining and decorating the chart pronouncing the familiar 'Two Days, Seven Hours and an Early Breakfast'. Some of these could easily have commanded a slot in the Tate Gallery.

But, generally, throughout the whole battalion, there was a very noticeable sense of apathy and boredom. Standards of discipline were nowhere near what we had been accustomed to during our training. But, then again, this was the real world. We were all here in position. This was not the time or the place for spit and polish. We were on the alert, poised, ready in case the Red Army should stream across the border. Here the RSM strode around the barracks puffing on a cigarette. It was like it must have been in the desert before El Alamein. There was no time for formalities.

Amongst the soldiers there was a new word which dominated and which illustrated the prevailing theme of the whole camp. It was another 'f' word and it might almost have replaced the original 'f' word were it not for the fact that it was almost invariably used in tandem with the original.

The new 'f' word was 'favourite'. Actually, it was really a double-barrelled word, 'fockin'-favourite'. 'Favourite' was the battalion expression describing any action that could imply avoiding some form of chore or duty. From brushing one's teeth in the morning, through the day's activities until last thing at night, there was a 'favourite' way of doing everything. It was the less arduous, corner-cutting method that was so admired by all. But it could be used to describe anything that was generally desirable. When correctly pronounced, 'favourite' could have the most salacious overtones. For instance, a good-looking female could be described as 'favourite'. The most 'favourite' of all would be Brigitte Bardot. Once, when duty officer, I had the misfortune to have to cope with the mutiny that broke out when the camp cinema was showing 'And God Created Woman', starring the aforesaid. Unfortunately, the projector broke down and I was forced to seek sanctuary in the sergeants' mess. When I explained to Peachey what had happened he described my predicament as 'distinctly unfavourite'.

One of the favourite occupations to while away the long hours was to visit the beautiful old city of Brunswick. Here we came into contact with the beaten enemy of the recent war. They were desperately poor and hung around the camp hoping for a Woodbine, or begging for a few pfennigs. Quite a few were offered some employment on the camp. Jobs that were considered too menial for the Brits were allocated to local civilian labour. Anything to do with sewage was distinctly unfavourite and was offered out to Germans. Many cleaning jobs, and even waiting in the officers' mess, were handled by locals.

For the soldiers, there was a favourite recreation at which they could pass many hours. They would go down to the railway station and start a tremendous brawl with the locals. These street battles were always referred to as 'Goodwill Missions' and they would frequently involve hundreds at a time and sometimes last all night. The military police would fly down in their jeeps to see fair play.

By way of partial justification for all this activity, it might be pointed out that it was only a short time since these same

Germans had caused us all a great deal of inconvenience and, in any case, they had their own way of keeping the score even.

In the city of Brunswick there were several streets which were the bastions of the German counter-attack. For the convenience of the Brits, they were all quite clearly marked out with large signs in English saying 'Out of bounds to all military personnel'. The most favoured street in this red light district was called the WinkelStrasse. Here the East Surrey Regiment pursued its other favourite pastime. There never seemed to be many casualties in even the grandest of the old-fashioned punch-ups. But every foray through the forbidden streets seemed to result in a vast increase in the workload of the poor medical staff back at the camp.

The real reason for our presence in Brunswick was hardly ever mentioned. Every two or three weeks we would take our turn at the frontier. Our real purpose was not so much to subdue the Germans but to monitor the activities of our co-occupiers from the Soviet Union. There were strict procedures to be followed and we spent several days at a time looking through a pair of binoculars at a pair of binoculars. We had to take note of every single development over on the other side of the border and all these reports were sent back to the War Office for evaluation. It is hard to differentiate which was the more boring activity, taking notes about the movement of one laundry van, or having to read and evaluate all this so-called intelligence. It was a sort of cat and mouse game about which no one could get very excited. It was not only that we were all complacent, it was also because we generally could not bring ourselves to dislike the chaps on the other side sufficiently. It was only a little while since these same fellows had been our great comrades in arms and, since that time, they had not really done anything to get us truly miffed. They had not dropped any bombs on us or raped any of our women. It was a lot easier to get on with our lives on our side of the border and focus our attention on the real enemy, the Duke of Wellington's Regiment, who were the only ones in BAOR who could seriously challenge the East Surreys' supremacy on the sportsfield.

14

A FINE MESS

It was not surprising that the East Surreys' married quarters sported some of the best looking women in West Germany. The regiment was blessed with some of the most dashing officers and men in the British Army.

After the war there had been a groundswell of admiration for our Armed Services. Not without justification, the Army was respected and admired as rarely before and never since. Many outstanding men had stayed in the Army after the war and many more had sought out the Army for a career in the immediate aftermath. Throughout the 1950s and 1960s the Regular Army offered a popular and flourishing career. Such uncharismatic figures as Field Marshal Montgomery were popular folk heroes and the whole nation watched with adoration as daring young pilots broke the sound barrier. The prestige of the Armed Services was probably at its highest level ever and young men strove to be considered as candidates. In the officer department, the supply of would-be candidates for Sandhurst far exceeded the demand. To obtain a cadetship at an officer training school was as difficult as entry to Oxbridge. The calibre of the resulting output was exceptional.

At the time that I joined the first battalion of the East Surrey Regiment, the establishment of young officers, the lieutenants and the captains, was probably as strong a group as was ever recruited into that regiment. They were the Young Turks of one of the finest armies in the world. They were career soldiers who were just beginning to climb the ladder of promotion. How sad to relate with hindsight that their chosen careers virtually evaporated around them as the Army and its prestige was cut back so drastically in the 1970s. Many of these men were the pick of the crop of their generation and they would be frustrated by the declining horizons of a military career over the next several years. The prospects of a glittering career subsided slowly over the subsequent ten years as the Armed Forces contracted again and again and they found themselves at the wrong end of a reverse pyramid of talent.

But all that was well into the future. In Brunswick, the Mole and I and the other national service officers were blessed with the opportunity to join these people through the back door, so to speak. They had committed their lives to the Army and had spent two years studying at Sandhurst. We were just amateurs, passing through, who had spent four months at Eaton Hall. Yet we held the same Queen's commission; we enjoyed the same privileges; we shared the same officers' mess. Instead of being greeted by superiority and resentment, we were welcomed enthusiastically into the community.

In total, there were probably nearly fifty officers in the camp. They were not all East Surreys, because there were several on attachment from other branches of the Service. There were medics and chaplains, chaps from the Education Corps, chaps from Intelligence and visitors from Brigade or Divisional HQ. There were about twenty national service officers, so there was quite a large percentage that the professionals had to tolerate. What's more, we were a shifting population, literally passing through. As some completed the two years and disappeared, so new ones, like Mole and I and, in another couple of weeks, David Ford, turned up.

The Mole had arrived before me and his reputation as a sportsman had arrived ahead of him. By the time I arrived he was already installed as quite a hero. His contribution around the cinder track at Hanover had helped the regiment to another stunning victory in the athletics championships and his prowess with the willow assured him of acceptance by all our fellow officers. By the standards of the East Surrey Regiment this rated him worthy of at least a Mention in Despatches.

Fortunately my reputation had not arrived ahead of me, so that I was greeted as something of a curiosity. For the first few weeks it was widely discussed behind my back in the mess that I either had some hidden sporting talent that was not being revealed for competitive reasons, or I was a spy from the War Office. When David Ford arrived, a couple of weeks later, it slowly dawned on the others that perhaps the colonel had not lost his marbles after all. There were times in the summer when virtually the whole establishment of young officers was absent from the camp for days at a time. This meant that some of the senior officers had to take on tasks that were quite unsuited to their status. While all the officers were wholeheartedly supportive of the regiment's commitment to winning every sporting trophy around, they had dropped the word to the CO that he might recruit one or two stooges who could look after the secondary duties that were beginning to become a bit of a nuisance.

When I arrived, there was a wonderful celebration taking place. The team had just arrived back from Hanover with the BAOR athletics trophy. The championships had lasted for nearly a week and the celebration lasted about as long. The whole camp thought this was 'Bleedin' Favourite', since most normal duties were abandoned to welcome back the conquering heroes. Most of the team were officers, apart from a few physical training instructors, so, in fact, Army duties went into abeyance for several days until the officers all sobered up. I imagined at the time that this was a very special occasion, roughly equivalent to VE Day and I threw myself enthusiastically into the spirit of the occasion. I soon realised, however, that, far from being a once-in-a-lifetime event, this was more or less a permanent state of affairs. The colonel, like a Roman Emperor, adored welcoming back his young lions from their latest sporting victory and, since the regiment swept the board at just about everything, we enjoyed a continuous celebration. Favourite!

Naturally the kingpin amongst the young officers was a sportsman. His name was Lt Tim Rogerson. His mates, everyone from the colonel down, called him Rodgy. His speed over 100 and 200 metres was breathtaking. He had a physique like a professional welterweight, which he might well have become had he not gone to Sandhurst, where he had been the *victor ludorum* incarnate. He left Sandhurst with a string of records and, naturally, joined the East Surreys.

Rodgy was a great sportsman. As summer turned to winter he would show what real pace and strength could do on the rugby field. But, most of all, he was a delight to be with. He was one of those whose sheer exuberance and energy lifts the spirits of all around him. He was the centre of every party; he was the perpetrator of every jape. He was loveable and crazy and as funny as hell.

Women adored Rodgy and so did men. The officers' mess adored Rodgy, but so did the sergeants' mess and so did all the men. 'That Mr Rogerson! He's well, favourite!' His reputation in the camp was secured for life when he met the most feared and hated man in the battalion in the regimental boxing championships. He met, in the final, the provost sergeant, Sgt Rippon. The provost sergeant is the head of the regimental police and his main duty is to beat people up. The Army recruits vicious bullies to do the job and Sgt Rippon was a class act. He was built like the proverbial brick outhouse and he had a first class degree in sado-masochism. When Lt Tim Rogerson met Provo Sgt Rippon in the finals of the regimental boxing, the big gymnasium was packed. Every soldier in the camp wanted to see this one. I sat next to the padre who nearly jumped into the ring in his excitement. It was the classic Beauty v The Beast contest and the Beast was murdered in three rounds.

Rodgy had a perfect stooge for all his jokes in the officers' mess and the two of them worked the double act in perfect harmony. Tony Ridger had been a contemporary of Rodgy at Sandhurst and they had joined the East Surreys together.

He came from a long dynasty of East Surreys. His father had earned a commission in the field and Peachey Oram was his uncle. He was as different from Rodgy as chalk from cheese. While Rodgy was hyperactive, Ridger was laid back. While Rodgy was all frenetic energy, Ridger was all quips and throwaway lines.

Some years after we met in Brunswick, several of us were in France on holiday. We had driven all night from Kingston and made a break in a small café in Montélimar. Because Rodgy was with us and he had been doing some of his usual acrobatic clowning we were greeted with a very warm welcome from M le Patron. Ridger was wearing an old beret à la Tony Swinson and he looked like Jean Borotra, so M le Patron assumed that he would be the natural translator. Accordingly, he put his arm around Ridger and embarked on a long oration, which was clearly addressed to us and was, presumably, some form of welcoming speech. After several minutes of his speech he paused and turned to Ridger to translate,

'Monsieur, here, wishes me to tell you that he has the longest tool in north west Europe.'

By way of irony, Tony Ridger later spent time in Cyprus during the Turkish/Greek war and discovered, almost by accident, that he really did have a gift with languages. He found that he could speak Greek fluently in no time. He was promptly sent back to London to develop this new-found talent and he was quickly able to master French and German as well as Greek and Turkish. He transferred to Army Intelligence and was posted to Northern Ireland.

Tim Ross was another regular officer and another who had been at Sandhurst with Rodgy and Ridger. He, too, was well qualified to be in the East Surrey Regiment, because he was another outstanding sportsman. He had already played cricket for the Army and he could turn his hand equally to both soccer and rugby. He was one of life's great companions.

Tim had all the qualifications to go right to the top in the regiment, but then tragedy struck. He had his leg badly smashed whilst playing rugby. He had stayed on in the Army because the medics hoped they could put him back together again. He had a series of operations, which resulted in him spending a lot of time at the depot. Each time his hopes were raised that the latest operation would do the trick and each time he was disappointed. He soldiered on, but it became clear that his career as a sportsman and as an officer was closed. Finally he was invalided out of the Army, but not until after we had got to enjoy his unfailing good humour. He had a crop of jet-black hair and an infectious laugh that made him irresistible to women. As Ridger was fond of observing, most of us might have been able to face adversity in the company of the succession of nubile blonde models that helped see Tim through all his suffering.

Rodgy, Ridger and Tim Ross were all lieutenants, that is, they had two pips on their shoulder. The national servicemen, like David Ford, the Mole and I, could only aspire to second lieutenant, but there was another full lieutenant who became a great friend. He was called Richard Bing and he had become a full lieutenant (extra 7s. 6d. per week) because he had signed on for something called a short service commission. He signed on for three years, as opposed to the two years that he would be liable to serve as a national serviceman. This meant that if, at the end of three years, he and the Army had formed some kind of mutual respect, he could carry on and become a regular. It also meant that he could be promoted full lieutenant during the three years. In the event, the Army did like Richard and he did carry on.

Dick Bing was a very elegant man who stood six feet two inches in his jungle greens. Like so many tall men, he was a truly gentle soul, but his height was used quite effectively in the second row for the regimental rugby team. He had a tiny little 'bubble' car, which he squeezed into and drove around the camp with his head sticking out of the sunshine roof. He had developed a unique way of returning a salute. A long arm would extend out through the window and complete a very smart salute outside the car, meeting a peaked cap protruding several inches out of the top of the car; a bit like a tank commander.

The British Forces had their own radio station in Germany, called BFN (British Forces Network). Every Sunday we listened to the BFN's version of Top of the Pops and Richard would conduct the chorus to the popular hits of the day. His speciality was 'Last Train to San Fernando' by Johnny Duncan and the Blue Grass Boys,

> 'Diddy, biddy, bum bum,
> The last traieeen to San Fernando.'

sang the whole mess, including the padre.

The commanding officer was Lt Col C. O'N. Wallis MC. The CO of a fighting battalion is a Big Cheese and Col Clive fitted the part beautifully. He was a big, bluff, handsome man, whose career as a back row forward for Ireland had been interrupted by the war.

Clive Wallis had been commissioned into the East Surrey Regiment in 1935, the same year he had played rugby for

Ireland. In 1938 he had gone with the 2nd Battalion to Shanghai. When all British troops were withdrawn from Shanghai in 1940, the 2nd Battalion, the East Surrey Regiment, was sent to Singapore and thence in February 1940 to Jitra in Northern Malaya. When the Japanese launched their lightning offensive through Malaya in December 1941, Captain Clive Wallis was the commanding officer of Charlie Coy.

At the Battle of Jitra the British were completely overrun and the East Surreys were cut to shreds. Nearly half their numbers were lost and those that survived struggled back through the jungle, with virtually no communications, paralysed by shock and fear, bewildered and exhausted.

The 1st Battalion, the Leicestershire Regiment suffered a similar experience, and the demoralised remains of the two battalions, the 1st Leicesters and the 2nd Battalion of the East Surrey Regiment, were thrown together in the field to form the British Battalion. Clive Wallis was appointed Adjutant and promoted to Major. It was this battalion, the so-called British Battalion, which fought so bravely at the Battle of Kampar, that the Japanese Command reported that they had met resistance from a totally new force which they believed to be a whole Brigade of Australians that had somehow arrived to reinforce the British and Indian forces. Quite why the Japanese thought they were fighting Australians has never really been explained. Perhaps they heard the lovely cockney of some East Surreys and mistook it for an Australian accent.

In any event, the British Battalion, though hopelessly outnumbered, brought the Japanese advance to a halt for the first time. At Kampar the entire Japanese 5th Division was halted in its tracks. Clive and his men, often cut off from each other, frequently with no idea who was attacking and who was being attacked, hurled themselves against the Japanese in desperate hand to hand fighting. Against a vastly superior force, in thick jungle, in clinging mud and in pouring monsoon rains, the British Battalion held firm.

Only when the Japanese landed below the British line did the British Battalion give up their positions at Kampar. There then followed the long, demoralising withdrawal to Singapore. On 15 February 1942 Singapore was surrendered. Clive Wallis was just twenty-eight years old. For his gallantry in Malaya, he was awarded the Military Cross.

In 1957 this great bear of a man was a batman's nightmare. Sometimes his appearance could get dangerously close to a shambles. On a hot day he would use his swagger stick to poke his huge peaked cap up off his forehead and he had a tendency to unbutton the top two buttons of his battledress tunic. Col Clive had a vast, jovial moustachioed face and he was a lovely, friendly man, much given to wrapping huge arms around his colleagues, especially when congratulating one of his beloved sportsmen. He had spent too much of the last war as a guest of the Japanese to dwell too much on the past. He saw life in the Army as an action business, particularly if the action was on the sports field. He was not too bothered about the namby-pamby, prissy business on the parade ground and even less about the text books which officers were supposed to study at Staff College. He was much more into action and slapping people on the back. His idea of truly uplifting and noble soldiering was to lead the senior officers against the subalterns in a game of indoor hockey in the officers' mess with an old beer can.

Unfortunately, Brigadier Freeland was not that sort of person at all and, even more unfortunately, Brigadier Freeland was our brigade commander and Col Clive's immediate superior. Col Clive was sporty and extrovert. The brigadier was cerebral and smooth. He was a brilliant career officer who was destined to reach the very highest echelon in the British Army. Col Clive might list his interests as sport, back-slapping and drinking, while the brigadier, even though he had himself been a notable sportsman, was more interested now in military history, strategy and politics. The two men were hopelessly incompatible and the rest of us were to become pawns in the conflicts between the two of them. Everyone expressed solidarity with Col Clive and, in deference to him, the brigadier was always referred to as 'The Smiling Shit'.

We all knew how much the colonel dreaded a visit from the brigadier and the brigadier, in turn, made it abundantly clear that he disapproved of the East Surreys and all their sporting trophies. The colonel's worst ordeal was when the brigadier made one of his fairly frequent and increasingly critical visits. It was part of the protocol that Colonel Clive would have to bring the brig into the officers' mess for lunch. All the officers would line up right across the full length of the mess and Col Clive would have to walk him along the line introducing him to all his officers, a bit like the captain of the team at Wembley. Unfortunately, the colonel had an absolute blind spot on names. Since there were nearly fifty of us and since the personnel changed on an almost weekly basis, this ritual could have been a bit of a challenge, even for memory man; for Col Clive it was an unmitigated disaster.

Clive Wallis could always remember one name. There was a captain called Tony Wade who, in some ways was a bit like the brigadier himself. I have no idea how Tony Wade came to be in the East Surrey Regiment. He wasn't a sportsman, nor did he seem to have any great interest in sports. He was a cracking efficient career soldier, who might easily have been a lecturer at the Staff College, a bit like a walking army manual. Because Col Clive relied on Tony Wade if he got any tricky problems concerning actual soldiering as opposed to rugby, he could always remember his name. Unfortunately, with the Smiling Shit standing alongside him, that was the only name the colonel ever could remember.

Down the line would go the duo with the brigadier shaking hands with fifteen 'Tony Wades' and another twenty-odd 'Tony Things'.

'Ah,' the brigadier would say in his so smooth, charming way,

'Another Captain Thing! How are you Thing?'

But then, at the end of the line, the colonel might occasionally be in luck. The favourite son of the East Surrey Regiment was called Hugh Greatwood. He was the captain of the Army rugby team, as well as the Inter-services shot put champion. He could drive a golf ball half way across the English Channel and was in every sense a true East Surrey. Unfortunately for Clive, since this was a name even he could remember, Captain Greatwood was not very often with the battalion since he was usually on urgent duty around the world leading some team or other into action. But, on those rare occasions he was present, the colonel puffed up with pride as he approached him on the end of the line up.

'And here, Brigadier, it gives me great pleasure to introduce Captain Greatwood, sir. He is the captain of the Army rugby team and captain of the Combined Services rugby team.'

'Morning Greatwood,' the brigadier would say curtly, and move on.

However, the routine continued. The absentee sportsmen continued to gallivant around Germany, sweeping up the trophies, while a handful of us doubled up duty after duty back in the camp. Occasionally the fixture secretary would fail to fill a day with a match, or a divisional trial or inter-company competition. But, even then, the teams were not permitted to take up any military duties for fear that some muscle or ligament might become overworked.

Fortunately for us, another national service officer appeared who had no pretensions to play anything at this standard, so David and I were able to share out some of the parades and chores. However, this new officer was an absolute case study for Major Earle's Man Management lecture. He was a classic loner who spent all his free time walking around the camp with a dog who had befriended him. There was something distinctly odd about his manner and it was not long before the combined psychiatry department of the officers' mess had come up with its diagnosis. He was homosexual. In the event our Man Management, when put to the test, fell way short of minimum standards. Even the chaplain seemed unable to broach the subject.

Then, suddenly, he disappeared. After a few days, Col Clive summoned all the officers to the mess. He told the hushed assembly that our recent new arrival had already left the East Surreys to join the SAS. The Colonel said he was unable to make any further comment. We were not to talk about it or mention his name ever again. Naturally, we assumed that this mysterious outfit called SAS was some kind of rehabilitation unit for homosexuals. Many years later I watched my television screen agape as men from the SAS, dressed in balaclavas and swinging on ropes, hurtled through the windows of the Iranian Embassy in London, hurling grenades. But, when the loner left, all David and I could think was that our duties would revert to their previous arduous schedule.

Then, the shortage of available officers became so acute that I was summoned to see the adjutant yet again. This time I was to add the duties of battalion weapon training officer to all the others I had already acquired. As with most of the others, my qualifications for this particular promotion were non-existent. The main responsibility of the battalion weapon training officer was to supervise all activity out on the range and to give instruction on how to shoot. It was generally helpful if the weapon training officer could himself shoot straight, whereas the merest glance at my record would have shown that I had only achieved a Grade Three. No one without a white stick fell into a lower category of marksmanship than Grade Three.

'Never mind,' said the adjutant with his usual friendly encouragement, 'there is no one else, so you will just have to do it. Go and find Cpl Hunter. He is the weapon training corporal. He will take care of you.'

One of the duties I had now picked up was responsibility for the battalion's ammunition. There was enough stuff in the camp's ammunition stores to make quite a large bang and this was where I found Cpl Hunter. 'Ammo corp' was a favourite job. No one was allowed into the ammunition stores without a special pass and this made the stores almost an inviolable retreat. Cpl Hunter was also the camp projectionist and, when I found him in the ammo store, he was just setting up one of his frequent unscheduled movie shows. There were several soldiers sitting in front of a blank screen while Cpl Hunter was stuffing a lot of notes into his pocket.

There were huge signs everywhere.

'NO ADMITTANCE' 'DANGER' 'HIGH EXPLOSIVE'.

Cpl Hunter greeted me with a cheerful wave,

'On for the show are we, sir? It's bleedin' favourite,' as he lobbed a fag-end over a pile of mortar bombs.

For the next three months I spent every morning going through my duties with my own company, and then Cpl Hunter and I drove out to the range, where one of the other company commanders would detach a platoon or two. It suited the company commanders because it kept their men occupied and, once on the range, they were my responsibility and not theirs. In addition, the soldiers found an afternoon out on the range was quite favourite compared to most of the alternatives. So there was no lack of demand for my services.

I soon got quite accustomed to giving lessons on a subject where my ignorance was on a grand scale.

'Squeeeeeze the trigger. Don't flinch.' That was about the totality of my weapon training instruction and I was always quick to volunteer Cpl Hunter for any practical demonstrations.

One day there was a particularly tiresome soldier who complained bitterly, and quite correctly, that the sights on his old shooter were all crooked. The men in the butts were working overtime with the little flag, or 'shitstick', which indicated that there was no mark at all on that particular target. We had a resident armourer, which was a bloomin' favourite job, back at the camp, but I remembered that he was flat out getting the movies together for Hunter's next show. So in a moment's aberration, I said, 'Give me the gun.'

In front of the whole platoon, I threw myself to the ground with the soldier's rifle and loosed off three shots in quick succession. There was a pause of only a matter of seconds before the little white disc that indicates a bullseye appeared three times and tapped the target.

There was a buzz of admiration all along the line and the platoon sergeant murmured, 'Fockin' fav'rit, sir', as I nonchalantly threw the rifle back to the amazed soldier. Only Cpl Hunter noticed that I had actually been aiming at the target two down the line from the one that showed the bullseyes.

But it wasn't just the old Lee Enfield rifle that was fired at the range. There was the Bren gun, which everybody likes, because it sits on its little tripod and doesn't recoil. And there was the Sten gun. The Sten gun is the one you fire from the hip, like Jimmy Cagney. This, too, was a weapon that was virtually obsolete and was shortly to be replaced by the Sterling sub-machine gun. But it was still in use up on my range and it nearly killed a number of us.

The Sten gun is supposed to be an automatic weapon, but the ones we were issued with had had a long innings and it was quite unusual for them to fire more than three rounds without jamming. To fire the Sten gun on the range it is very important that the firers stand in a line across the range. On the command, they advance together remaining abreast and at right angles to one another. The range then produces a number of targets in the form of cut-outs representing terribly ugly soldiers simulating the position they would take to fire at us. As the firing squad advances along the range, the targets suddenly jump up out of the undergrowth and that is the signal for rapid fire from the hip. The potential for disaster is without parallel on the range. Bullets fly in all directions, but very few hit the ugly buggers. Most of the guns jam, at which point the soldier is supposed to follow a very strict procedure, pointing the gun at the ground immediately ahead. But, in the excitement of playing Jimmy Cagney with live ammunition most soldiers elected to abandon this procedure.

'Oi, sir, this bugger is jammed,' they would cry as they turned the thing directly towards me, or the man alongside.

'Ooh, it seems OK now.'

It was not only shooting. There were other activities we were called upon to teach where our own skills were deficient. All the physical training instructors were in the athletics team and most of them were professional footballers. So, like nearly all the junior officers, they could not perform their duties for long stretches of time.

One time David and I, as usual the only two junior officers within several miles of the camp, were sent off by the adjutant to take two platoons out on to the athletics practice area and give lessons on various aspects of field and track. The colonel wanted to make sure that he left no stone unturned in his search for hidden talent. Captain Wade nominated David to take one platoon off to practise sprint starts and baton changing, while I was sent off with the other platoon to the long jump pit and the pole vault area.

No amount of bluff could convince any member of my platoon that I knew anything about pole vaulting, so kindly Sgt Puttman suggested we just move over to the pole vault area out of sight of Captain Wade and have a smoke. This seemed the favourite thing to do and we all settled down for a puff and a chat, when I suddenly heard a terribly familiar voice.

'Now then, Brigadier. What have we here to look at? Why here is young Mr Thing teaching his platoon to pole vault.'

By this time every member of the platoon was up on his feet and jogging up and down loosening up. To my horror I heard the colonel desperately trying to explain to Brigadier Freeland, who was on one of his surprise, unannounced visits, why the mastery of pole vaulting was such a valuable military skill.

'Jolly good,' said Colonel Clive, as he desperately stalled for time. 'You see being able to pole vault is absolutely essential for a soldier for er . . . er . . .'

The colonel's cerebral pulse worked overtime and produced inspiration,

'Er, yes. For escaping from a prisoner of war camp.'

The Smiling Shit rolled his eyeballs skywards.

'Well, get on with it.' He looked at me with irritation surging through every pore in his body.

I looked at Sgt Puttman in desperation and the kindly sergeant elected to keep his eyes fixed on a small leaf at his feet. He shrugged his shoulders.

I walked forward two steps smartly. I bent down and picked up the pole. It was two and a half miles long and it bent in the middle making it extremely difficult even to walk. I looked like a set of weighing scales as I trudged back fifty yards along the run up. When I turned to face the apprehensive faces in the distance, I think I said under my breath,

'Now look here, platoon. I am now going to demonstrate the pole vault.'

With Colonel Clive and the brigadier on one side, and Sgt Puttman and the whole platoon lining the runway on the other side, I set off.

I recalled reading somewhere that the key to success in the pole vault is speed down the runway. So I accelerated along the track, moving smoothly through the gears until my little legs were flying round at maximum revs. All the time I was

trying to control the wretched pole, which insisted on sway-
ing up and down from end to end. As a result, the business
end of the pole dug itself into the ground a little earlier than I
would have planned.

Undeterred by this premature take off, I rapidly adjusted
to the new time scale and leaped into the air with all my
might, expecting to find myself flying skywards. I recall a
great sensation of burning hands as I hurtled along the length
of the pole and then there was a very loud clattering sound as
I fell head-first into the sandpit.

15

A MOLE GOES TO WAR

Whether it was as a result of my demonstration of the pole vault, we will never know. It might have been because of some other shortcomings the brigadier had spotted on his snap visit. But the edict that arrived from brigade HQ was uncompromising and quite devastating.

The first battalion of the East Surrey Regiment was deficient in all aspects of its training. Until such time as brigade HQ, i.e. the Great Smiler, was satisfied as to our standard of military efficiency the whole camp would be withdrawn from the frontline. We were banned from competing in all sporting activities. The whole battalion, without exception, would move out to the great training area at Sennelager for a month of arduous field exercise, followed by a series of tests in which the capability of every officer would be assessed. Then, after a month under canvas, the battalion would be required to take part in a brigade exercise devised by the brigadier, which would simulate a full-scale nuclear war. Only if we could satisfy brigade HQ during our participation in this exercise, would we be allowed to return to Brunswick and compete again in sports.

The significance of the name of the exercise was not missed by Col Clive and the rest of us. The exercise was to be called 'Final Match'.

They were dragged back from the cricket pitch and the hockey pitch. Cricketers who had been playing at brigade and divisional level were sent urgent messages of recall. We even came back from the ranges. The balloon had gone up.

The CO addressed a stunned officers' mess. We had been rumbled. The game was over. There was nothing else for it. We just had to put the tracksuits away and put on uniform and buckle down. The colonel added a few favourite words about the Smiling Shit, but that was it.

I glanced at David, who sniggered a little. I glanced at Mole. He was ashen-faced. Most of the other officers just could not believe what they were hearing. The East Surrey Regiment not play games! Preposterous! That's what we were here for! This was a bit like telling the England football team they all had to join the civil service! It was unthinkable. But it happened. I saw officers that day I had not seen for months. Tony Jacobsen had joined us the same day as David Ford, but I had probably only seen him twice in as many months, because he was another soldier sportsman. He was a wonderfully athletic, blond, Scandinavian all-rounder. He would later open the bowling for Oxford University, but, right now, he looked as shattered as the rest. Wicketkeepers and goalkeepers, hookers and strikers, pole-vaulters and hop, skip and jumpers, they were suddenly all in the same boat. Where had they left their uniform? What was all that they learned about platoon in attack at officer school? Indignation was the order of the day.

The trucks rolled out of the camp all day, headed for the Sennelager training zone. Sennelager was Germany's answer to Salisbury Plain and it stretched for miles between Bielefeld and Paderborn. This was the playground for most of the British Army of the Rhine. Not only did the Poor Bloody Infantry crawl on their stomachs all over this area, but here, too, were artillery men firing off their great, noisy guns and armoured divisions cruising around in their smoking, clanking tanks. There were traffic jams of armoured cars and the whole heath swarmed with soldiers, guns, mortars, tanks, anti-tanks and air support. It was no picnic on the heath. My dear, the noise! Even at night the noise was quite breathtaking and the sky was permanently illuminated with flares, Very lights and rockets.

Not only were we on enforced manoeuvres, but we were on trial as well. The brig had made it quite clear that he was dissatisfied with the level of our skills and with the standards of our leadership at every level. Everyone was under examination, from the CO himself to the lowliest corporal. But it turned out that the people who were most on trial were the platoon commanders. In the infantry, which is the backbone of the British Army, the platoon is the basic unit and the brigadier had told the colonel that he particularly wanted to see the platoon commanders operating in all conditions, the more stressful the better.

Platoon commanders only really do one thing in wartime, or certainly on exercise, and that is 'the platoon in attack'. The manuals don't devote much space to 'the platoon in retreat', so we just had to practise platoon in attack until we were blue in the face.

(In case the exercise is still classified, I would ask all Russians, or other potential enemies, to skip the next paragraph or two.)

The platoon commander, second lieutenant, deploys his three sections in preparation for attack. Each section is commanded by a corporal and each section has a two-man Bren gun team. The Bren gun team should have the basic skills to fire the gun and is usually under the command of a lance corporal or a very trusted private soldier. According to the topography, two sections are deployed either to the right or the left of the third section, which retains the services of the dashing young subaltern. The two sections then dig in and select their firing positions. Usually this is supervised by the platoon sergeant, who remains in overall command of the firing squad. The third section then sets off in the direction of the enemy position, usually employing 'the leopard crawl'. When the platoon commander's section gets within a short sprint of the enemy, the sergeant orders the other two sections to open up rapid fire, preferably on the enemy. As a hail of fire pours into the enemy position, the platoon commander breaks cover and, usually brandishing a pistol and crying out Henry V's speech at Agincourt, he leads his section, who have fixed bayonets, in a furious attack on the enemy. At this point the firing squad is supposed to maintain the level of fire to keep the maximum pressure on the enemy, but the arc of fire should move slightly to the right or left, according to the direction of the platoon commander's charge, so as to avoid striking your own men. After a brief hand-to-hand combat, the enemy is wiped out and the subaltern gets the MC.

Needless to say, it doesn't always work out this way. It particularly tends not to work out this way on exercises when the platoon is using live ammunition and when Col Clive is sitting immediately behind the lines observing Brigadier Freeland observing.

I am preparing my final assault when I hear above the din of my firing squad,

'Mr Thing! Your Bren group is the wrong end of this section. Their angle of fire is across your riflemen. They should be at the other end.'

From a distance of at least thirty yards, I yell across to No. 2 Section Bren group, trying to make myself heard above the scream of rapid fire,

'No. 2 Section Bren group. When I say "Move", move to the other end of the section. Now, "Move!"'

I was gratified to see the Bren group had heard me. Cpl Ernie Barrett, whose civilian occupation was a street trader, and Pte Leroy Smith from Jamaica picked up their Bren gun and ran the whole length of the section right in front of the firing squad!

We also had to practise platoon in attack at night, using tracer bullets and flares. This could also produce a certain amount of confusion in the ranks. But this was small beer compared to the confusion that could come about on some of the other exercises, nearly always under the watchful eyes of the top brass. Some of these exercises were a mixture of Boy Scouts and party games, but, because the whole battalion was on trial, it was all taken desperately seriously.

One of the most demanding of the platoon commanders' tests was the operation of a snatching party. It was a well-known fact that, even in a time of nuclear war, the Army had to maintain the necessary skills to pluck an individual out of enemy positions and bring him back through the lines. Here he would be interrogated so ferociously that he would reveal the enemy's code for pressing the nuclear button. This was done by a 'snatching party' and, of course, this dangerous and skilful task was the job of the platoon commander.

The brigadier was especially keen on this exercise and each of us was to be tested in 'snatching'. All this had to be done at dead of night and under a starless sky. The brigadier placed men from his HQ around the field to act as observers and report on our success or failure. While members of one platoon prepared to play the part of the enemy, the platoon commanders of the other platoons blacked up with boot polish and selected their most trusted NCOs to make up the snatching party.

When all was in place the colonel selected the first party to crawl out into the pitch darkness and grab a prisoner.

'The first to go will be 2nd Lt Hole,' said Col Clive.

This was partly because the Mole was one of the few names that the colonel could remember and partly because he wanted to start with a strong card. If this exercise was all about speed across the ground and strength in the attack, he knew he could rely on one of the best athletes in the battalion.

The plan was fairly straightforward. Watches were synchronised. The platoon commander picked three of his best men, usually two young corporals and a thug. They would crawl out in to the darkness, across enemy lines and, hopefully, right up to the enemy trench. At a prearranged time, the rest of the platoon would create a diversion. This consisted of firing rifles, shooting rockets, banging saucepans and generally making an unholy racket, which would petrify the enemy lying uncertainly in his trench. At the moment of maximum distraction, the platoon commander and his trusty snatching party, who had infiltrated the innermost parts of the enemy position, would seize one of the enemy and dash back across the lines. The whole snatch would take seconds only and required a combination of agility and split-second timing.

Once the prisoner has been grabbed, he is frog-marched in double quick time back through the enemy lines. He is grasped firmly between two of the snatching party, one on each arm. The snatchers then run at a furious pace, holding the unfortunate prisoner facing backwards from the direction in which they are travelling. In this position the prisoner is supposed to be so stunned and so disorientated that he is incapable of any resistance.

2nd Lt Hole was blacked up and his beret was pulled charismatically over his eyes. He and his snatching party were only lightly armed, but lithe and loose as they stepped out into the pitch darkness.

At absolutely the right moment, the rest of the platoon suddenly erupted into a cacophony of screaming, firing and hurling thunderflashes and then, just as suddenly, fell back into a total silence.

There was a pause of nearly twelve minutes during which no one breathed. The tension back at HQ mounted as we all waited anxiously for the return of the gallant snatching party. Then, somewhere out there in the darkness, there was the sound of scuffling feet and heavy breathing. They were hurtling back from the great snatch.

'But, sir! But, sir! . . .' the prisoner was whingeing as he was dragged backwards at a frantic pace over the uneven surface. There was a hissed response from one of the snatchers under his panting breath.

'Shut up, you,' followed by the sound of a sickening blow.

Still no one stirred back at HQ. Unusually for Sennelager, there was a total silence during which we could hear the approaching party surging across the heath and dragging their reluctant prisoner. Another minute passed.

Then, quite suddenly, the group burst into our presence and fell, heaving and panting in a heap at the very feet of Col Clive and the brigadier.

'But, sir! But, sir! I am one of your men,' said the prisoner.

Once again, the Smiling Shit's eyes rolled heavenwards as the dreadful truth dawned. 2nd Lt Hole had snatched his own man.

In many ways, my own attempt at the 'snatch' was even more bizarre than the Mole's effort. By the time my turn came, several hours had elapsed and dawn was just about to break over the great Sennelager training area. This was a slight disadvantage to the snatching party because we would be more visible from the enemy trenches as we swept in for the *coup de grâce*. Frankly, I saw it as more of an advantage as I had been very unsure if I could have located the enemy in the pitch dark. Also I knew that it was largely my own platoon under Sgt Puttman who was playing the role of the enemy, which meant that I should be able to distinguish them from the snatch party. It also meant that, after lurking in their trenches all night, one or two of them might just be flagging in their watchfulness. By now I had become fairly aware of the fortitude and commitment of my own platoon and I guessed that, after a long night of banging and snatching, one or two of them might be snatched in their sleep.

I selected two corporals and Pte Leroy Smith as my snatching party, thus putting a slight premium on athleticism over intellect. The two corporals and I blacked up, while I barked out orders in my most authoritative voice. Because we were going to crawl along a ridge alongside the woods to our left, so as to avoid any risk of detection, I gave instructions that we would keep in touch with each other by a hand signal every twenty yards or so. Then we stepped out into the night.

After the first leg, I looked backwards over my shoulder. The emerging dawn gave just sufficient light to allow me to make out the three dark figures crawling behind me in single file. I raised my right hand as the signal and each of the snatch party acknowledged in turn with the same little wave of their right hand. So we progressed slowly around the ridge and in the lee of the trees. Every twenty yards I repeated the hand signal like a Red Indian and each time I saw my three men wave back.

As we approached the enemy position we made even slower progress, as we all crawled even closer to the ground trying to eliminate every sound of our movement. This whole mission could be destroyed by the crack of a twig or the rustle of a leaf.

I looked back over my shoulder for what seemed like the hundredth time to signal to my men and check their position. The first corporal was now quite clearly visible just a few feet behind. He raised his hand to acknowledge my signal. Behind him I could see Leroy also raise his hand and then, further off, but just visible in the first light of day, I saw my second corporal raise his right hand. My three-man snatching party seemed to be in place.

But then, to my complete amazement, another hand rose up out of the darkness even behind No. 2 Cpl. I stared into the gloom and there, about fifteen yards behind me, I could quite definitely make out a fourth figure crawling along behind. I must be hallucinating. The pressure of these tests must have overtaken me. I decided the only course was to ignore this phantom and crawl on.

We advanced another twenty yards or so and my heart was beating loudly as I turned to repeat the hand signal and wait for the acknowledgements. One after another the hands were raised. One, Two, Three, Four. This was totally baffling. I decided that there was only one thing for it; I must crawl back, retracing my steps and investigate. I could just about make out the incredulous expression on the blackened face of the first corporal, as I whispered to him that we seemed to have picked up a stray. I crawled on back past the other two men and still the interloper seemed to be attached to my snatching party. I withdrew my pistol from its holster and prepared to challenge the impostor.

'Christ, Tony, what on earth do you think you are doing?' whispered a gentle Scots burr.

Cameron Boyle had been in the same squad as Webby and David Ford at Eaton Hall and I knew him quite well in those days. But what the hell was he doing here in the middle of Sennelager in the middle of the night, in the middle of my exercise? Second Lt Cammy Boyle was with the Cameron Highlanders. Not only was he in the wrong exercise, he was in the wrong regiment. I was incensed and I was explaining my dissatisfaction to him in a stage whisper when yet another complete stranger turned up.

This one was one of the brigadier's stooges who was play-ing umpire on our exercise. Cammy and I buried the hatchet and froze as he approached. The newcomer was wearing the white armband of an umpire and was carrying a torch. It was a real testimony to our stealth that the wretched umpire practically stepped on Cammy without seeing him or me. It was not until it became all too obvious that he had not seen us and that he was just about to relieve himself on us that we broke cover. A stream of Scottish curses and a lot of pompous gesturing by the umpire were greeted by complete disbelief by the rest of my snatching party, who were still maintaining cover in the darkened undergrowth.

Needless to say, all this unexpected activity aborted our snatch and led to a full-scale enquiry when we returned to HQ. Apparently, Cammy Boyle had been taking part in some totally separate exercise with the Cameron Highlanders. He had got a little disorientated and then a little weary. Suddenly, he woke up in the field to see three dark figures crawling along, so, naturally, he tagged along behind. But criticism was fairly liberally thrown around in the colonel's post-mortem. Even the umpire, who turned out to be some rather feckless major in an obscure tank regiment, did not escape his share. There are some fairly strict rules governing calls of nature in the field and he had failed to follow the procedure. He, in turn, claimed that he was not a participant but an umpire and therefore not subject to the rules of engagement.

Cammy Boyle and I were singled out for criticism on a higher charge. According to the colonel, we were seriously at fault in breaking cover when under threat from the umpire. It was tantamount to cowardice in the field to take evasive action and we should have remained in position in silence throughout and suffered the ordeal. Cammy was escorted back to rejoin the Cameron Highlanders. Apparently they were so pleased to see him back that they all embarked on a typical Scottish celebration. He was totally exonerated and the Camerons sent a sharp note through brigade HQ complaining that I had mucked up their exercise.

Needless to say Cammy also turned up at Cambridge

after the war, where his skills on the rugby field and in the boxing ring became interchangeable, which reminded me how dangerously I had lived out there in Sennelager when I risked provoking someone who would later pack down for Scotland.

The brigadier and his stiffs from brigade HQ monitored our other exercises as well. Signals exercises are very easy to monitor, because it is easy to tune your radio on to the same wavelength as the battalion and eavesdrop on every exchange. In fact the whole principle of signals is that that is exactly what the enemy is going to do. Even though we could very rarely hear much of what was being said, we had to assume that the enemy could. For this reason we all had to learn elaborate procedures and codes to ensure security.

'What ho, Tone. Mole here. Tell Rodgy the old bastard is looking for him,' would not do at all.

This should be, 'Foxtrot Delta, Foxtrot Delta, calling Alpha Charlie. Are you receiving me Alpha Charlie? Over.'

'Alpha Charlie, Alpha Charlie, this is Alpha Charlie, I hear you Foxtrot Delta. Over.'

'Foxtrot Delta, Foxtrot Delta, this is Foxtrot Delta. Tell Bluebell, Sunray is looking for him. Over and Out.'

Each of us had a call sign with which to identify ourselves, but to confuse the enemy. A commanding personage is always called Sunray, whether he is a lance corporal or a field marshal. One must never disclose a rank as this would be a fatal breach of security. If the enemy were to hear any reference to a rank, it would, of course, immediately reveal the size of the force opposing him. If he picked up over the air reference to a major, he would know that a company was in the field; a colonel and he would know there was a battalion around; a corporal and he would know less than a dozen men were at hand.

While all this security could lead to a certain amount of

confusion, it was greatly exacerbated by the poor standard of our signals equipment. This was before the days of tiny, hand-held radios that can transmit to the moon and back. We were using wireless sets that weighed about fifty pounds and had the range of only a few hundred yards. They were operated by two heavy batteries the size of an old car battery. Each platoon had a poor, unfortunate soldier designated as signals operator. This was emphatically not a 'favourite' appointment. The signals operator had to run around the battle ground with a thing on his back like a camel's hump and, to make him even more visible to the enemy, he had an aerial like a fishing rod sticking out of his head. The first rule of engagement was always to shoot the platoon commander, but the second favourite was always the signals operator.

In the heat of battle these two men would frequently be squatting side by side, thus offering the enemy the opportunity to kill two birds with one shot. The platoon commander would hare across the open terrain and dive for cover in some shallow ditch. Then, in the best British Movietone News tradition, he would call out, 'Sparks!'

Usually, the poor signals operator, weighed down by the enormous pack on his back, was several hundred yards behind, dodging a hail of bullets and weaving from side to side. When he finally arrived at the side of his platoon commander, he was so top-heavy that he would fall on top of him. Even then, it would be quite impossible to either receive or transmit until the duo had moved to a piece of high ground, preferably away from any sort of cover. This is one reason why radio messages in the field tended to be fairly brief.

On signals exercises, however, the signals equipment was mounted on the back of a jeep or an armoured car and all the officers would fly around in their vehicles communicating with each other on the radio. Occasionally, through all the hissing and bleeping, we actually picked up a few words. However, the slightest obstacle, like a building or a tree, would soon obliterate this. Just in case we might start enjoying this particular exercise, Colonel Clive briefed us and reminded us that the brigadier was sitting in at his convenience, listening to our every word.

A and C companies were driving up the middle of the battlefield and B and D companies were sweeping up the flanks, driving the retreating and scattered enemy before them. Or, at least that was the imaginary scenario set by the colonel. In spite of a lot of buzzing and crackling on the radio, we mostly seemed to know what was supposed to be going on, with the possible exception of the Mole. Mole's signals skills were probably a bit rusty, because there had not been much call for them out on the cricket field. David and I had given him a quick refresher course and we had advised him to keep well clear of the colonel's big armoured car and stay out of range.

Mole's call sign was Foxtrot Delta and I immediately felt a ripple of concern when I heard Sunray himself asking over the air for Foxtrot Delta. A very familiar voice, but with a slightly irritated tone, was repeating,

'Foxtrot Delta, this is Sunray. Come in Foxtrot Delta. Come in Foxtrot Delta. Over.'

There was a very remote hissing sound but no real indication what had happened to Foxtrot Delta. That is, until I could see Mole's jeep quite clearly in view only about fifty yards away from my own position. Even without my binoculars, I could see the Mole sitting in the passenger seat of his jeep, chatting away into his microphone, quite oblivious of the fact that the only sound coming out the other end was a distant hiss. Perhaps, I thought, he had encountered some freakish atmospheric conditions, or else, God forbid he had forgotten to turn his wretched set on, or he was tuned in to the wrong wavelength.

Then suddenly all became clear. Mole had parked his jeep right at the foot of a huge electric pylon. No wonder his transmission was about as audible as a lizard's fart.

I had just asked my driver to take me over to the Mole so that I could warn him that he was not in the favourite position for the best reception, when my earphones were practically blown off the side of my head.

'Look here, Foxtrot Delta! Get away from that pylon! I said GETAWAYFROMTHATPYLON! You . . . Over,' screamed the colonel into his radio.

And then the big armoured car came hurtling into view. My driver swerved violently to avoid being run down by the great truck. Smoke poured from beneath the huge ridged tyres of the colonel's armoured car, as it raced across the terrain, bouncing over the boulders, towards the little jeep under the pylon.

All the time Sunray was broadcasting a string of obscenities directed at Foxtrot Delta. All the time Foxtrot Delta was chatting amiably into his mike.

'FOXTROT DELTA, LOOK HERE, THIS IS SUNRAY. GET AWAY FROM THAT F . . . ING PYLON.'

I saw a look of sudden apprehension on the face of Foxtrot Delta. He snatched up his microphone and the whole exercise and the brigadier heard a slightly wavering voice make the fatal security mistake.

'Er, Foxtrot Delta. Er, which Sunray is this? Over.'

I had no need of my radio to hear the colonel, by now incandescent,

'This is God Almighty F . . . ing Sunray,' he screamed, 'now will you GET AWAY FROM THAT PYLON!'

'Foxtrot Delta. Message received. Roger.' Mole's jeep shot out from under the pylon like a hare breaking cover.

'And DON'T ROGER ME!' screamed Colonel Clive.

16

FINAL MATCH

Exercise Final Match was to have been the culmination of all our efforts at Sennelager. We had spent nearly a month under canvas and morale was edging lower by the day. It was now mid-September and the weather was beginning to turn nasty on us. No one had mentioned to us that there was a monsoon season in West Germany. But, as we entered the countdown for Exercise Final Match, the Heavens started limbering up.

The day the exercise was scheduled to start I was awakened by torrential rain in my little tent. The torrential rain was indeed *in* my tent, because so much rain fell in the early hours of the morning that the little bivouac, that had been my bedroom for the previous month, just collapsed on top of me. I managed to disentangle myself from the clinging wet canvas and peered into the early light. The whole tented camp area was a quagmire. Mud and derision stretched across the whole area. As I struggled to my feet, most of the first battalion the East Surrey Regiment was pursuing some variation on the same theme. I saw David Ford, who had been occupying the next tent. Unlike mine, his tent seemed to have survived intact, but he was standing alongside it in sodden pyjamas.

'Bleedin' favourite!' he said. 'These tents are really water-proof. Once the water gets in, there's no way of getting it out.'

Alongside the tent that used to be the officers' mess, a little stream was winding downhill into the adjoining field and a procession of laundry and personal belongings was being swept along by the quickening tide. Everywhere I could make out the figures of disconsolate soldiers paddling in the great flood. This was not a propitious start to the three-day/three-night exercise, which the brigadier had named Exercise Final Match.

The officers had their own dugout latrines. Very exclusive. These consisted of a long trench above which was a series of cubicles separated by a piece of damp hessian cloth hanging from broken wood.

I made my early morning pilgrimage full of trepidation about the coming exercise. I always found the total lack of privacy a bit of a restraining factor, but, on this occasion, I was even more inhibited when suddenly the bit of hessian was ripped sideways and Rodgy's cheerful face poked around the corner into my cubicle.

'What ho! Good luck with the exercise.'

I was uncertain which exercise he was referring to as I was already having some difficulty completing this part of the exercise when I heard a familiar 'plop, plop, plop' from the adjoining cubicle.

'Lucky sod,' I said through gritted teeth.

'Luck nothing,' called out Rodgy. 'I just dropped my knife, fork and spoon.'

The real exercise itself turned out to be cold, damp, muddy and a complete disaster. In one regard only could anyone claim any degree of success for the exercise. In war, real war, there is a very high element of chaos and confusion. In this respect, Exercise Final Match was totally realistic. For three days and three nights neither I, nor anyone else I came across, had the slightest idea what was going on.

This was a brigade exercise so all the units in the brigade were involved. As well as three battalions of infantry, there were tanks, artillery and even air support all contributing to the congestion and confusion on the sodden Sennelager training field. This meant that a total of nearly five thousand men were committed to Exercise Final Match, but only about half a dozen knew what was supposed to be taking place.

The brigadier had devised this whole complex exercise. High on his list of objectives was the humbling of Col Clive and his battalion of dilettante sportsmen. Unfortunately, the East Surreys were already designated as scapegoats for anything that might go amiss in the next three days. Since it was to transpire that the whole exercise would be an unmitigated disaster, the poor East Surreys were heading for one of their biggest defeats since 1825 when the troopship 'Kent', in which half the regiment was embarked, caught fire and foundered on its way to India.

The commanding officers of each of the participating units were summoned to the highly secret exercise briefing at brigade HQ. Such was the level of secrecy attaching to this briefing that each CO was allowed only one other officer from his unit to attend. In an attempt to comprehend some of the detail, Col Clive rolled the dice and took Captain Wade to the briefing. Most of the other COs took their second-in-command, but Clive knew that Tony Wade was about his best shot if the brigadier started to get technical with map references or wavelengths.

It very soon became clear that the gamble had failed on this occasion. Such was the bewildering sequence of tactical and technical instructions that were thrown out by the brigadier and his staff, particularly in the direction of the East Surrey contingent, that neither the colonel nor Tony Wade was able to grasp the exact detail of the exercise. In general outline, the exercise was to simulate a full-scale response to an attack by the Russians. In the course of their attack, the

Russians would fire several tactical nuclear missiles, which would make a large part of Sennelager into a fairly uncomfortable zone. The instructions included a bewildering array of details of radiation levels, responsive strikes and compass readings.

After two hours of concentrated briefing, the brigadier adopted one of his beatific smiles, looked around the packed room and asked if there were any questions,

'East Surreys, OK?' he said smoothly.

'OK, sir,' said Clive promptly, while Tony Wade looked at him in disbelief.

They then stumbled out of the brigadier's mobile HQ with a look of complete incomprehension on both their faces. However, the fact that our representatives at the briefing had not understood one word became the least of our problems. There then began the Army's own game of Chinese Whispers. This is when each commander passes on instructions, which he didn't understand in the first place, to the next in line. The CO, immediately on his return, summoned the second-in-command and his three company commanders to his briefing. With Tony Wade at his elbow, poor Clive tried to recall something of the gist of the brigadier's instructions. Occasionally, Tony Wade would interject when he thought the colonel's orders were becoming particularly fanciful and this would lead to an altercation between the two of them.

Then the company commanders passed on the Chinese Whispers to their three platoon commanders. The quizzical expression on the face of our company commander as he struggled to make sense of the orders he had received was sufficient warning to all of us that some of the finer details might have already escaped along the way. In turn, I knew we were in deep trouble when I passed on the few smatterings of my orders that made any sense to Sgt Puttman and my three section commanders. What they passed on to their gallant warriors bore no relation whatsoever even to what the colonel had told his company commanders, let alone what the brigadier had originally conceived.

We set out at first light for our first nuclear war. Sgt Puttman and I looked knowingly at each other. This was going to be a complete buggers' muddle. Sgt Puttman had twenty years experience, including the total chaos of a real war, and so he was more accustomed to the feeling of complete helplessness as we marched out to take up our position at the designated map reference.

The platoon was carrying so much equipment that there was a distinct ring of Barnum and Bailey as we trudged out of the morass that used to be our tented camp. Not only were we each carrying full battle gear, but we also had shovels and mortars, camouflage nets and wirelesses. And, in addition, we had to carry the full paraphernalia of nuclear war. Each of us had our all-over radiation suit, which weighed another thirty pounds and was strapped to the back of our packs, along with a gas mask and a steel helmet. Armed to the teeth, we were quite incapable of fighting anyone.

We were headed for a map reference that was, to say the least, a bit controversial. The instructions had been quite clear, we were to head for this grid reference and dig in. However, there was a lot of confusion about the map reference. If we had followed exactly to the spot I was given, we would have marched about five hundred miles into the Eastern Zone, so I had used my initiative in massaging the map reference and assuming that the 'T' in my code was in fact a 'J'.

This was the reason that we dug in on the edge of a small German housing estate. Because of the confusion surrounding my orders as they related to this position, our support truck did not locate us for the next forty-eight hours, which might have meant that we had to survive with no rations for that time. But it was not only our support truck which failed to find us; neither did anyone else. My instructions had stated that, after a few hours, a squadron of tanks from the third Royal Tank Regiment would join up with my platoon and we were then to form a combined operation. No such event took place.

We were totally forbidden to break radio silence, so all we could do was to dig in and concentrate on making ourselves as comfortable as possible. We had one stroke of good luck when Cpl Barrett found a couple of German road menders and negotiated to borrow their pneumatic drill. While the compressor roared noisily, we managed to dig some very satisfactory trenches. Cpl Barrett managed to design a drainage system that helped to remove some of the hundreds of gallons of rainwater that continued to fall. We may not have been precisely on the position that the brigadier had intended for us, but we had the most comfortable, best camouflaged suite of trenches in the whole exercise. It seemed that the tank commander had completely failed to make his meeting with us and we were also untroubled by any other visitors. Even if anyone had been sent to look for us, they would have had the greatest difficulty finding us. Our subterranean warren was almost totally concealed by camouflage netting and undergrowth. We could move around between the three trenches without breaking cover and Ernie Barrett was well on his way to his first Mention in Despatches. We may have left our hand grenades in our support lorry, but he had brought enough sets of playing cards to allow three separate poker schools to get under way. He had opened negotiations with the civilians in the housing estate nearby and exchanged Woodbines and other military equipment, that seemed to be superfluous to our immediate needs, for food and drink. He had also rigged up some very superior latrines and Sgt Puttman had put up little bog-roll holders.

Exactly when the Russians launched their first nuclear strike we never knew. Sgt Puttman, drawing on his years of experience, persuaded me that our correct course of action was to lie low. If our lack of activity should be called into question, we would claim we were taking appropriate precautions for a radiation alert.

Then, after nearly two days, there was a development. A small British Army jeep pulled up and parked just outside our housing estate. A figure covered from head to toe in his radiation suit climbed out and plodded slowly towards our position. Sgt Puttman woke up our sentry, who grabbed his rifle and poked it out of the trench.

'Halt! Who goes there?' he cried out at the approaching figure.

To my astonishment, I heard the gentle Welsh lilt of the battalion chaplain.

'Only me, boyos,' sang out the Rev Captain Olwyn Jones.

Sgt Puttman whispered noisily in my ear,

''Ere, sir. It's the f . . . ing padre!'

Was this a trick? Had the brigadier set this up to trap me?

I snapped out to the sentry to hold him right there, while I climbed out of my trench, with my pistol at the ready.

''Ullo boyo,' said the chaplain, as he recognised me. ''Ow you doin'?'

I wasn't falling for this one.

'Hands up,' I snapped. 'Now put your hands on the back of your head and move slowly to your left. Now, Move!'

The poor padre looked distraught, but followed my instructions. He inched carefully to his left towards the sentry.

Suddenly, there was a Welsh scream and the Rev Jones disappeared.

He had stepped on the brush covering of Cpl Barrett's trench, which was supported by nothing more than a camouflage net. He crashed downwards on top of No. 3 poker school to be greeted by howls of awful blasphemy.

We soon established that the padre was just the padre and he was not one of the brigadier's stooges in disguise. He was able to tell us that the first tactical nuclear weapon had exploded some three hours ago. It had scored a direct hit on our little housing estate and apparently the map reference, which we had been given by mistake, was the actual drop zone of the first nuclear strike. The Rev was going about his spiritual duties in accordance with his instructions. He was moving through the radiation area delivering the last rites to any survivors.

While I consulted urgently with Sgt Puttman, three poker schools looked on uncomprehendingly while the chaplain moved amongst them murmuring his blessings. The good Sarge and I were unsure how we should proceed. According to the rules of the exercise we were all dead. Furthermore, the lads had settled in to quite a comfortable routine in the trenches and it was still pouring with rain outside. We could just accept the worst and be dead, or we could gather up all our kit, leave our nice, dry position and march several miles through impenetrable mud and probably get hopelessly lost trying to find the rest of the battalion. All in all, being dead seemed favourite.

But this tough decision was made for us. Even as Sgt Puttman and I were wrestling with it, another Army vehicle pulled up alongside the housing estate. This was a ten-ton truck and it disgorged several very noisy uniformed men, who ran across the little patch of spare land that separated us from the housing estate, bawling and shouting at us. This was very obviously a cadre of the brigadier's stooges and they were showing very little respect for the dead.

My whole platoon was dragged out of the trenches and lined up in single file like prisoners of war. The senior umpire formally notified us that we had dug in at the very spot where the first nuclear warhead had exploded. Therefore we would not be permitted to play any further part in the exercise.

On this bit of news, there was a murmur of approval from the ranks. However, being dead turned out not to be such a rosy option after all. We marched nearly ten miles with all our kit and in the pouring rain. We were not repatriated with our own battalion, but we were incarcerated at brigade HQ. We then had to wait during the entire duration of the exercise, sitting on a wet and greasy bank, exposed to the elements.

Only when the referee blew the final whistle on Final Match were we allowed to return and rejoin the East Surreys. My platoon had played a rather undistinguished Final Match and I was fearful that we might be subjected to unjustified criticism on our return. But, in the event, the performance of the whole battalion, in fact of the whole brigade, had been so poor that we were not singled out for any particular blame. The exercise had been one big chapter of accidents. One whole company had got completely lost and had spent two whole days and two whole nights paddling aimlessly around the Sennelager training area, trying to make contact with the rest of the battalion. They had finally run into the first battalion of the Duke of Wellington's Regiment and mistakenly attacked them.

But the incident which the brigadier himself chose to highlight in his debriefing, which was conducted before the whole battalion, involved David Ford.

David Ford was a platoon commander in the company which was under the command of Tony Wade. Captain Wade was the one man in the Surreys who might reasonably be relied upon to make a good showing on exercise. He was an officer with real pretensions to command, which he combined with more than a passing knowledge of tactics. Furthermore, he had been at the original briefing at brigade HQ and had got his confusion straight from the horse's mouth.

Tony Wade's company had been singled out to play a very prominent part in the whole exercise. On the third day, it would fall to him to lead his men on a daring exploit. They had been selected to establish the beachhead, which would be the pivot to the whole counter-attack that would turn the battle in our favour. This could only be undertaken after a squad of specialists had raced ahead to de-toxify the territory from the effects of radiation. In the event, the nuclear specialists had failed to make the rendezvous and Captain Wade and one other officer had very bravely undertaken the task themselves. All this had caused some delay in the main operation and it was not until late on the third night that Tony Wade was able to summon his platoon commanders to his HQ for the crucial briefing.

By the time Captain Wade was preparing for his drive into the very heart of the enemy, he and his troops had been in the field without rest or sleep for the best part of seventy-two hours. One of his platoons had been wiped out in a minefield and the strength of his company was drastically reduced. But he was a true professional and he was determined to demonstrate to brigade that at least someone in the East Surreys was battle-hardened and serious.

It was about 3 a.m. when Captain Wade assembled his little 'O' Group. He had only two platoons to carry out this important mission. One was commanded by a young national service officer called Alan Duvivier and the other was commanded by David Ford. These were the two officers who were summoned, together with their platoon sergeants, to receive Captain Wade's orders for the attack. They were crouched attentively in the bottom of Tony Wade's trench when the brigadier himself appeared, together with a little posse of his staff, to eavesdrop at this crucial time.

Captain Wade was a model of efficiency. In a voice tense with anticipation, he whispered his orders to the occupants of the trench while Brigadier Freeland listened from above. His five-minute briefing was detailed, clear and precise. There was a brief pause as the captain let his subordinates digest his instructions and then, he looked towards Alan Duvivier,

'Any questions, Alan?' he whispered.

'No, sir. All clear, sir.'

He turned to David,

'Any questions, David?'

There was not a sound from David.

'Any questions, David?' repeated Tony Wade, with a note of urgency creeping into his voice.

There was a long snore from David.

'David! Wake up. You bastard.' It was too late. The Smiler rolled his eyes skywards.

Exercise Final Match Replay began five days later.

17

BACK TO BRUNSWICK ANNAT

After Exercise Final Match, the whole brigade was castigated like naughty schoolboys and the brigadier demanded that the complete exercise be repeated.

The second time around, there was a marked improvement. The weather cheered up no end and quite a few of the participants seemed to understand what was supposed to be happening. And those that didn't, which again included my platoon, managed to conceal their ignorance from the brigadier's men.

When the colonel announced that we had all passed the test and we were now allowed to return to the frontline, the whole battalion breathed 'bleedin' favourite' with one collective sigh of relief. An entirely different mood overtook everyone as we prepared to strike camp. No unit has ever returned to the frontline with such an outbreak of joyfulness. Peachey ran around under a cloud of cigarette smoke, cracking jokes even with private soldiers, and Colonel Clive congratulated everyone and practically knocked me unconscious with a huge slap on the back.

The soldiers packed up their hated tents and flung them

gleefully in the back of the waiting trucks. They were elated at the prospect of returning to see all their friends back at Brunswick, especially those whose address was 'Out of bounds to all military personnel'. The best address in this little complex was the WinkelStrasse. They sang,

> 'It's a long way to tip a Brigo,
> It's a long way to go
> Farewell Sennelager, Goodbye shitty dump,
> It's a long, long way to tip a Brigo,
> But the old fool won't jump.'

Other verses developed the theme as to where they would like to tip the Brigo and compared the exercises at Sennelager with those they were planning to perform in the WinkelStrasse.

The prospect of walking away from the dirty, muddy Sennelager training area and returning to the luxury of our Four Star barracks was truly uplifting, even if the real enemy was a lot closer at Brunswick than at Sennelager. It was a rousing, singing, laughing convoy of trucks that streamed up the autobahn carrying the East Surrey Regiment back to Brunswick.

When we got back, the local people of Brunswick were genuinely pleased to see us. There was a positive explosion of goodwill down the WinkelStrasse and the lord mayor invited all the officers and their wives to a welcome-back reception at the Town Hall.

The reception was a grand formal event. All the local dignitaries were invited and all the officers and all their wives dressed up in their best finery. We were all paraded in our best mess kit and, as soon as the party got under way, the booze was flowing like water.

Unfortunately, things nearly got out of hand.

Colonel Clive was in one of his most expansive moods. When the lord mayor arrived, the colonel was surrounded by a bevy of truly gorgeous wives and was giving a not altogether accurate account of the heavy defeat he had inflicted on the Red Army out at Sennelager. When the lord mayor introduced his refined and elegant young wife to the colonel, Clive threw his great arms around her and slammed a huge moustachioed kiss on her upper lip. Mrs Mayor seemed to recoil a bit from the colonel's enthusiastic greeting, but he just put it down to the fact that she had not yet had a drink. With a cheery wave he summoned over the nearest young officer, who happened to be Tony Ridger. He passed the mayor's wife to him like a birthday present,

'Here,' he said in a very audible whisper, 'loosen her up a bit. Give her something to drink.'

The lord mayor spoke impeccable English, but his wife didn't. But Ridger was not deterred. He thrust a very large glass into her hand and steered her away from the CO. The two of them started to engage in a kind of sign language and it soon became clear that the mayor's wife was discovering what the rest of us all knew, that Tony Ridger was a very funny man. Even in sign language, he was witty and there were soon great peals of laughter coming from their direction.

Meanwhile Colonel Clive enormously enjoyed introducing all his female company to the lord mayor. Somehow he seemed to have a much better grasp of the names of the wives than he did of the husbands, or maybe it was because he was not having to make introductions to his great nemesis, the brigadier. As each young wife was introduced, each one received the added bonus of a huge hug from the colonel. None of them showed any objection. Not only was the colonel boss to each one's husband's, but he was an extremely handsome figure in his blue dress uniform. And the party began to gather pace.

Ridger was obeying the CO's orders to the letter. There

seemed to be an almost continuous procession of waiters fill-
ing up glasses in their corner. Several of the waiters seemed
to be wilting with exhaustion from rushing back and forth to
the bar to refill the glasses of the jolly couple. But not Ridger
and Mrs Mayor. Their sign language seemed to be bordering
on the hysterical and the lord mayor glanced across a little
apprehensively at the shrieks of laughter emanating from that
corner of the room.

'Salut!' said Ridger as he raised his glass for the umpteenth
time.

'Shlut!' said Mrs Mayor with a giggle. 'What you say in
Ingleesh?'

'Oh,' said Ridger, 'cheers usually.'

'Cheershushally!' said Mrs Mayor. 'What elsh you say?'

'Oh,' said Ridger, a little absent-mindedly, 'Good Health!
Bung Ho! Bottoms Up! Up your Flue!'

Mrs Mayor seemed to focus only on the last of Ridger's
suggestions. 'Up your Flue!' she cried as she downed another
massive drink.

At this point Ridger rather lost control of his charge, who
seemed to be suddenly fired with enthusiasm for her new
vocabulary. She positively tore across the room towards the
group, which included her husband and Colonel Clive and,
with a look of absolute triumph in her eyes, she raised her
glass.

'Up your Flue!'

She went on a walk-about around the now silent room,
with Ridger nervously in tow trying to restrain her.

'Up your Flue!' She raised her glass to the wife of the Rev
Captain Olwyn Jones.

It is occasions such as this that separate professional
soldiers from mere national servicemen and fortunately
Rodgy was on his mettle. With a brilliant ploy he distracted
everyone's attention while Ridger was able to get back in
control. He snatched up a soda siphon and moved to the

end of the bar. Here there was a little washing up basin for the staff to wash the glasses and, in a flash, Rodgy had positioned himself opposite. He leant against the wall with one arm and turned his back to the room, while concealing the soda siphon, which was in his other hand. The terrible silence that had descended on the room was interrupted by an even worse noise.

The whole assembly was stunned to hear an appallingly familiar sound. There was a quite dreadful hosing noise coming from Rodgy, followed by a sort of urgent rushing noise as the pressure was released from the soda siphon. Colonel Clive's jolly expression gave way to a look of absolute horror as he was confronted by the awful prospect that one of his officers might be committing the only crime worse than desertion in the face of the enemy. Everyone in the room felt embarrassment crawling insidiously through their body. The lord mayor looked as if he was about to pop out of his great chain of office.

Rodgy swung around to face the audience with a sheepish grin on his face and a soda siphon in his hand.

'Sorry, sir. The siphon got jammed,' he said.

The sigh of relief that swept around the room was greater even than when the brigadier had said we could leave Sennelager. The CO stepped forward and gave Rodgy a slap on the back of Olympian proportions. The look of consternation on the mayor's face was replaced by a wide smile, even though his wife was still repeating to all and sundry,

'Up your Flue! Up your Flue!'

But Rodgy's diversion had done the trick.

Eventually, we all recovered from the celebrations of our return to Brunswick and we settled back into the routine of occupying ourselves with drills and practices around the camp. The one big difference from the situation, which had existed before we all went off to Sennelager, was that we had just about twice as many officers working as before. The total ban on sporting activities had been lifted, but, for the first few weeks anyway, the colonel thought it would be advisable to turn down some of the invitations to compete. No longer was the battalion being officered by a few senior officers, plus David Ford and me. No longer did I have to spend every afternoon at the ranges at Wolfenbüttel.

In fact, there were now so many officers around that the adjutant was slightly stressed to know how to deploy them. Each company was commanded by a major, but now, in our new embarrassment of riches, each company was allocated a captain to act as second-in-command. I was still working under the same company commander, who was a wizened little veteran called Major Ashby, but now we were joined by Captain Geoff Strong.

The reason Geoff had not been much in evidence in our former life was because he was a runner, not a sprinter, but a distance runner. So he had been a leading member of the battalion athletics team. Geoff had been a training officer at Eaton Hall when we had been there and Mole and I had met him there when we were trying to gain acceptance to the East Surrey Regiment. We all knew that Geoff was on an upward career curve, because only the best regarded officers got sent to do a tour of duty at Eaton Hall.

The first time I ever saw Geoff Strong was at Eaton Hall. He was running cross-country. There were dozens of people jogging around the grounds at Eaton Hall, but this was not what Geoff was doing when I first saw him. He was pounding across the uneven field, dressed in black shorts and a black singlet. There was a large white competitor's square on his vest with an equally large number and a sponsor's message. In his hand he held a stopwatch, which he glanced at every few strides, as he strode out, with flecks of sweat drifting across his face. Geoff was an Army cross-country champion and was close to international honours.

He was also a superb regular officer and now he had joined my company as second-in-command. He made it clear that he saw his task as raising the standard of the company. He wanted to improve the discipline and the appearance of the whole company, including the junior officers. The only trouble was that Geoff was blessed with a wonderful sense of humour. He was married to the beautiful Maureen and, of course, he was also away a great deal with the athletics team. This meant that we had not seen much of him around the officers' mess. On those few occasions that he had been in the mess, he had been a constant delight with his wealth of funny stories and absurd poems, which he could recite for hours. With only the slightest encouragement, he could recite all twenty-eight verses of 'Eskimo Nell' and his repertoire extended to most of the sonnets and verses penned by the Masters.

Even though Geoff was a captain and we were only very lowly subalterns, he soon became a good friend in the mess, which might have made it a tad difficult when he came to join my company and made it clear that he was going to take a bit of a grip.

However, I did what Geoff wanted as well as I could and, in fact, I found myself welcoming the slight quickening of the tempo, which followed his arrival. My only real fear was that Geoff might make me laugh in front of my platoon. However, both he and I managed to keep a straight face and it was quite clear that all the company including the officers and the NCOs had properly noted Geoff's arrival.

Inevitably, it was Geoff himself whose straight face would crack first.

The company sergeant major in our company was called CSM Washington. He was very tall and rather spindly. In fact he was a rather incongruous figure who looked a bit like a stick insect. He also irritated Geoff for some reason. I think Geoff thought he was a bit slack in his discipline and that he was too much of a crony with the other three sergeants in the company. But no one, not even a zealous new second-in-command, has a head-on confrontation with a CSM. So, the activities of the company proceeded, but with relations between the second-in-command and the company sergeant major remaining a bit strained.

Not only did CSM Washington have inordinately long arms and legs, such that, when he saluted, he looked a bit like a dragonfly, but he also had an absolutely infuriating verbal habit. He simply could not open his mouth without adding 'Annat' at the end of every sentence. In fact, frequently he could not even wait until the end of the sentence. This particularly got on Geoff's nerves. It seemed to him to be lacking in the sort of military precision expected of a warrant officer to add 'Annat' to just about everything.

'Good Morning, sir, Annat.'

On the parade ground I would see Captain Strong positively wince as his CSM would call the company to attention.

'COMPANEE . . . ATTEN . . . SHUN. Annat.'

There was very little that Geoff could do about it, because this had become an affliction with the poor man, but, of course, the soldiers all went around cruelly imitating the CSM. Washington-Speak prevailed throughout the company and it was altogether prejudicial to good order and discipline.

Matters came to a head when the company clerk reached the last day of his national service. His seven months, three weeks, four days, five hours and an early breakfast had reduced to just the five hours and an early breakfast. End-of-term exuberance led him to type up that day's company orders in Washington-Speak.

0630 hrs Reveille . . . Annat.
0730 hrs Breakfast . . . Annat.
0815 hrs Company Commander's Parade . . . Annat.

And so on, throughout the notice of the day's activities.

Major Ashby was on leave and Geoff Strong was acting company commander. He had summoned his three junior officers to a meeting in the company commander's office. He was addressing us from behind his desk when there was a knock on the door.

CSM Washington burst in with a look of extreme indignation on his long face. It was rather clear that the good sergeant major was not well pleased. He pounded his ungainly legs to attention, saluted his rather wobbly salute and addressed himself to the acting company commander.

'Good morning, sir. I have to report, sir, that the company clerk, sir . . .'

I could see Geoff counting the pauses and waiting for the dreaded 'Annat'. Then he raised one eyebrow and started nodding with approval as the CSM moved through the syntax without a single 'Annat',

'. . . has typed up company orders, sir and he has typed Annat at the end of every line, sir . . . Annat.'

Regrettably Geoff could not conceal his mirth.

18

ANOTHER FINE MESS

I began to thoroughly enjoy my activities with Sgt Puttman and my platoon. I no longer had to spend half my day pretending to be the weapon training officer, because there were suddenly more than enough officers to go round.

As a matter of fact, Sgt Puttman himself had been a fairly consistent absentee in the pre-Final Match days, because he was the only non-commissioned member of the battalion cricket team and, therefore he had been off playing cricket for much of the time. He was a real East Surrey insider. He was a veteran of the war and had several yards of ribbons on his tunic to prove it. In his youth, which had been quite a few years previously, he had been the East Surrey heavy-weight boxing champion and his fellow sergeants still called him 'Slugger', because that was what he had been apparently. Now, in his more mature years, he had made quite a name for himself as the regimental wicketkeeper. He wasn't especially good, but what he lacked in general mobility and skill, he made up in courage. Actually it may have been more stupid-ity than courage, but he let through surprisingly few byes. He always insisted on standing up to the wicket, even when he was keeping to the quicker bowlers. He would even try to stand up to Tony Jacobsen, who was distinctly quick. A phalanx of young officers would stand in a row of slips, a good two paces to the rear of Sgt Puttman. As the ball hurtled past the surprised batsman, the keeper would make very little effort to move his gloves to the ball, but he rarely failed to have the rest of his body behind the line. The ball would strike the keeper a sickening blow on the body, or even quite frequently, on the head.

'All right, Sarge?' the slips would call out in unison.

'Sir. Right, sir,' would come the reply, as Sgt Puttman picked up the ball and lobbed it to mid-on and prepared to receive the next delivery.

Now, however, the cricket season in Germany had come to an end and Sgt Puttman was devoting more of his time to platoon duties. He spent much of his time in friendly competition with a sergeant in one of the other platoons in our company, called Sgt 'Topper' Brown. Topper was a much younger man than Sgt Puttman, but they were both rogues who enjoyed their off-duty life together, especially around the bar in the sergeants' mess, where the favourite pastime was to lure the young officers to a liquid fate. The duty officer was always expected to make a late night call on the sergeants' mess. This was a mixture between a courtesy and a brush with certain death. Technically the young officer was supposed to close the bar! In fact, there was no way a young subaltern would prevail over up to forty or more sergeants and sergeant majors to close their bar. Instead the RSM would stand the first round and would then look around for that particular officer's platoon sergeant to 'entertain' him, while the bar stayed open. Sgt Puttman and Topper Brown worked as a team. No one survived their attention and I was at a real disadvantage because Sgt Puttman was my platoon sergeant. In other words, when I was on duty, they rubbed their hands in anticipation.

Topper Brown had started life in the regimental band, as he was a competent player of several instruments. But after a minor altercation with the bandmaster, he had taken his musical talents elsewhere in the battalion and turned up as one of the platoon sergeants in my company. He played a mean saxophone and he sang a bit.

In the sergeants' mess he had a little group that played on almost any pretext. Whenever I had the misfortune to be on duty, I could be sure that Topper would be blowing up a storm for the benefit of the sergeants and their wives and girl-friends. These were not the sort of parties that stopped dead when some little wimp of a subaltern walked into the mess and started stammering, 'Er, I say, Er, etc.' The RSM who, of course, was far, far senior to a junior officer was always the very soul of politeness, but the basic weapon was always the same: booze and plenty of it, to keep the duty officer quiet.

I really liked Sgts Puttman and Brown when I was stone cold sober but, when I was duty officer, I used to discover that I absolutely adored them. The real strength of the two was that, the next morning on parade, they would never make any reference to the appalling condition of their platoon commander the night before. Their professionalism was demonstrated by their ability to draw a complete veil over even the most bizarre and unfortunate performances.

Just as I was beginning to enjoy my duties with Sgt Puttman and his mate, I was suddenly and quite unexpectedly pulled away. I was summoned by the adjutant and told to report to Major Bishop. The adjutant was himself called Bishop, so Major Bishop was always referred to by his initials, which were S.C.A.N., to differentiate him from the adjutant, who was Captain D.R. Bishop. When I was told to report to 'Scan' Bishop, I could not avoid a slight tremor, just a hint of trepidation. Scan Bishop was a man with a fearsome reputation.

He had arrived less than a month before, but his reputation had come well ahead of him. Most of the senior officers

who had served with Scan spoke about him a great deal, long
before he arrived and they always spoke of him in reveren-
tial tones, almost with bated breath. Some of the stories we
had all heard about Scan Bishop were truly daunting. He
was a true tough guy. He had been captured by the Japanese
in Hong Kong and had then survived the full term in the
appalling conditions about which we are still being made
aware. He survived by being tough, wiry and obstinate. His
bravery bordered on insanity. His particular speciality was
an almost superhuman physical fitness. He made his name
by asserting that every officer should be able to undertake
every task that might be demanded of any of his men on the
field of battle and always be able to complete it quicker and
better. He seemed to take his own philosophy to extremes
and some of the stories we heard about his physical endur-
ance were little short of terrifying. From all I heard, he
seemed to spend most of his life on an icecap in nothing
but a jockstrap, or else engaged in unarmed combat with the
physical training instructors.

After the war, he had found life in the peacetime Army
with the East Surrey Regiment was a little soft for his taste,
so he had been seconded to the Parachute Regiment where
he was more comfortable with the sort of daredevil soldiering for which the Red Berets were renowned. Even the
Parachute Regiment had found some of Scan's exploits a bit
extreme, but he soon seemed to command the same respect
from his fellow Parachute officers as from the senior officers in his own East Surreys. I remember well the eager
anticipation with which the news of Scan's reappearance
had been greeted. It was widely assumed that the brigadier
had secured his return to the battalion to add a little fibre.

When Scan had finally turned up at Brunswick, he arrived
in a swirl of dust and a shriek of brakes. He drove his beloved
open-top Sunbeam Talbot, in which he had won some quite
important victories in various races. As befits a professional

daredevil, he wore goggles and an Army issue leather tunic. I remember thinking that Biggles had arrived.

When he dismounted, he turned out to be quite small in stature, bald and bespectacled. He looked more like Clark Kent than Superman and in his manner too, he seemed to me to be quite different from his reputation. On the few occasions I had seen him in the mess, or around the camp, he was always a little reserved and withdrawn. In spite of that, he maintained an unusual degree of respect from his fellow officers. He was the only person, other than the brigadier, who brought all conversation to an immediate halt as he walked into the mess. While we were quite used to the brigadier's icily charming request that we should, 'Carry on and just ignore me', we were quite unused to Scan's rather embarrassed little nod of acknowledgement as he moved across to the far side of the room to pick up a newspaper.

However, as I was to learn shortly, no sooner had Scan arrived than he was off again. The only potential problem was that I was off with him. We were going to Bury St Edmunds in Suffolk. What's more, Bury St Edmunds was to be a frontline posting, not because the Red Army was camped in the next field, as was the case in Brunswick, nor because the natives were getting restless. Apparently the War Office had decided to withdraw the first battalion, the East Surrey Regiment from Germany and place us in a sort of contingency reserve back in England. We were to be an emergency strike force, standing to arms, ready to be flown into action in any trouble spot that might arise anywhere in the world.

Scan Bishop was given the job of making the arrangements to withdraw from Brunswick and to take up position in Bury. It was a classic example of the pleasure the Army takes in miscasting people. Scan was an action man, better suited to hand to hand combat with Zulus than pen-pushing and logistics such as this job required. He wasn't a f . . . ing staff officer, as he told me. He was absolutely fuming. It was a bit like putting Errol Flynn in charge of choir practice.

But that was the job he had been given. He was allowed one junior officer to help him and he gave me absolutely no explanation why he had chosen me. Frankly, I was terrified of him. I found this silent ex-war hero a bit daunting at the best of times. Under the pressure of this unwanted job, he seemed quite likely to explode with anger and I didn't relish the opportunity of being his assistant.

But that was the job I had been given and the two of us set up office side by side and started drawing up lists. We had lists of everything. There were lists of personnel, lists of supplies, lists of transportation, lists of ammunition and lists of lists. Paper was everywhere. This was the last possible job in the British Army that Scan would have countenanced. He cursed his luck and reminded me constantly that he should have been leaping out of an airplane, or driving cold steel into some Fuzzy-wuzzy. And yet we gradually got to grips with it and I came to realise what a supreme organiser this man of action had become. We worked around the clock and I realised slowly that I was working with a thoroughbred. He never missed a detail and he never lost his quiet sense of humour. In spite of his absolute contempt for the job he had been given, he executed it with a relentless efficiency.

After about a month we had prepared everything for the departure from Brunswick. The next stage was to prepare for the battalion's arrival the other end. Scan and I would be the Advance Party. My return from Brunswick to the UK was in marked contrast to my outbound journey. Instead of travelling on public transport, with three convicts and a madman for company, I pulled on my goggles, climbed up alongside Scan in his Sunbeam Talbot and prepared to roar down the Autobahn.

Scan thought he was at Brooklands as we hurtled across Europe in a cloud of dust. Scan just lived in the fast lane and he celebrated his liberation from the hated paperwork by driving recklessly and delightfully at the speed of light. One night we stopped at a mess belonging to a Divisional HQ, which was formal and boring, so Scan decided that we should detour for our second night. The Sunbeam raced through a whole series of small villages and came to a halt outside a little inn on the Dutch border beside a whispering stream in the depths of the countryside. Here we spent an exhilarating and drunken evening where Scan and I talked long into the night about his addiction to adventure and his life of madcap heroics. Genuine warmth had developed between us.

The camp we had to possess at Bury St Edmunds was called Blenheim Camp and was still fully occupied by the first battalion the Argyll and Sutherland Highlanders. They would return north of the border and the plan was that our lot would return from Brunswick and walk into or, more correctly, march into Blenheim Camp three days after the Argylls had departed. In those three days the advance party had to prepare everything for the incoming battalion. Signs, colours, flags had all to be changed. The whole barracks had to be transformed in preparation for the new arrivals. To assist us in this formidable task, the regimental depot assigned to us one colour sergeant, two corporals and five private soldiers, but they would not arrive until the day the Argylls moved out. Until then, Scan and I were on our own. We actually had to take up residence with the Argylls for three weeks to complete a hand-over/take-over exercise on the whole camp and its contents. We had to sign for every building, every stick of furniture and every piece of equipment.

I was a little concerned that these Scots folk might not take too kindly to a couple of intruders whose job was to audit everything and check that it was in good order. In spite of all Scan's heroics, he was quite a little fellow and I was similarly impaired. I had visions of huge hairy blokes in kilts giving us rather short shrift.

I need not have worried. Soldiers have an innate sense of respect for one who has distinguished himself on the field of battle. Scan was a walking insurance policy. I don't know how the Argylls knew of Scan's war record, and indeed no one ever referred specifically to it, but somehow I just knew that they knew that Scan was the real thing. We were welcomed with open arms.

I had the good fortune to spend a little time as a guest of one of the most famed regiments in the British Army and I was able to bathe in the reflected glory of the East Surreys' be-medalled war hero. The culmination of our stay with the Argylls was an invitation to be honoured guests at the Mess Night at which the Argylls celebrated their imminent return to their homeland. An evening of swirling pipes, shouts and reels never to be forgotten. At the dinner table the Argylls' CO proposed a toast to the East Surrey Regiment and presented Scan with a little engraved silver cup to be added to our mess silver collection. And the old warrior replied to the toast with all his gritty charm, as the pipes and drums prepared to play our regimental Quick March.

The following day I had been delegated by Scan to do the takeover of the cookhouse and rations. I stood in a dark, freezing store like an audit clerk with a little clipboard, peering up at thousands of rashers of bacon. My eyesight was slightly defective from the previous night's celebrations. My opposite number, from whom I was supposed to be taking over all these stores, stood about six foot three inches and had the typically Scottish name of Frans ten Bos. Before too long he too would represent Scotland on the rugby field.

I just signed.

As the Argylls marched out behind their pipes and drums, Scan took the salute.

We then had just three days to have everything prepared for the East Surreys. It was hectic but successful. Scan presided over every detail and when the lads arrived it went without a hitch.

Colonel Clive marched up the hill to Blenheim Camp, accompanied by Captain Greatwood carrying the regimental Colours. Then all four companies marched behind Bandmaster Snowden and the regimental band. They swept into Blenheim Camp, where Scan was standing to attention on a little rostrum. There was a broad smile on Colonel Clive's face as he returned the salute.

Truck after truck drove into the barracks and every one was greeted by a member of the advance party and directed to its destination. The entire battalion marched straight into new quarters. The wives and children moved into the married quarters, the sergeants' mess was in action by six o'clock that evening and the bar opened in the officers' mess half an hour later. The regimental colours were decorating the dining room and all the regimental silver, including the latest acquisition, was on display. Drinks were on the house for the advance party who were the heroes of the hour. Just three days after the Argylls marched out, the East Surreys were in position.

We had a wonderful reunion and heard all the stories of the great withdrawal. One well-known sergeant had bought a second-hand Mercedes car in Brunswick and obtained special permission to drive it back to Blighty. Unfortunately, when he arrived at the Hook of Holland, which was the point of embarkation for the return, he was told by a customs officer that he had to pay an import duty that was slightly more than he had paid to buy the car in the first place. Since he did not have the money and, since he was a bit incensed, he drove the car off the end of the quay. Apparently it made quite a splash.

The regimental band tried to smuggle cigarettes into the country. The contraband was concealed in every one of the band's musical instruments. This might have escaped detection had not one of the customs officers given the big drum a playful tap and noticed a dull thud. There were twenty thousand cigarettes packed inside.

One or two of the soldiers did not want to come home. A couple disappeared the night before departure. One of them never did turn up and there was some concern that he might have nipped across the border into the eastern zone, but the other one was found by the military police three days later in the WinkelStrasse in a very exhausted condition.

19

GODSPEED FROM THE COCKEREL

All these minor transgressions were soon forgotten as we all settled into the luxury of a home posting. Even though we were supposed to be in a more or less constant state of Red Alert, we were able to settle quite quickly into a familiar routine. Just across the road from Blenheim Camp was a golf course, the rugby team started to get into training for the Army championships and there was even a spot of home leave at the weekends.

And then, on top of all this frontline soldiering, the East Surrey Regiment found time to make the news; not once, but twice in the space of less than six months, we would appear on the big screen at the Odeon. In between the 'B' Feature and the main film, the cockerel of the Pathé newsreel would crow from a little triangle mid-screen, while the miracle of cinema technology surrounded him with four different action pictures on a split screen. Then the headlines of the week, with just a little padding from the previous week, would be narrated in a fixed monotone that conveyed the timeliness and the urgency of the story.

Admittedly the first time we featured, we only made a

few screens in East Anglia, but the second time it was the full treatment, nationwide. Furthermore, the second time, Colonel Clive himself was up there in black and white on the big screen, slapping the interviewer on the back and practically knocking the microphone out of his hands. Then they put on the old 33⅓rd rpm Pathé Action record in the background while the narrator used his flattest, most stirring voice to say,

'And we all wish the brave men of the East Surrey Regiment, Godspeed and all success on their vital mission. We all want to join the Prime Minister in his good wishes. Good luck and thank you, the East Surreys.' Captions roll, cockerel crows,

'Cock-a-doodle-doo'.

The reason we made the newsreel the first time was because of our participation in an engagement that came to be called 'The Battle of Six Mile Bottom'.

The winter of 1957–8 was a tough one, especially out there in the wilds of East Anglia. There was frost and ice during all the early months of 1958. We were training in some really severe weather to keep the troops finely tuned in case we should be called into action at any time. We remained fighting fit and on high alert, but, in spite of our preparedness, the call never came. Then, right at the end of the long winter, towards the middle of March, the great global crisis occurred.

A train on the main London to Newmarket line got stuck in the snow at a junction in a village called Six Mile Bottom. So heavy was the snowfall that it had proved impossible to get the emergency services in. There were just four passengers and a driver on board and, after failing to rescue them, the Newmarket Fire Brigade had called the Government for assistance. The Government called the War Office and the War Office called Colonel Clive. The crack infantry battalion on emergency standby went straight into action.

When the call came it was quite late on a Friday evening.

Several were on leave and those remaining had been having a fairly spirited time in the NAAFI. Topper had been holding one of his hops in the sergeants' mess and, even in the officers' mess, there had been a fairly lively end-of-week dinner.

Two companies were mobilised in a matter of minutes. Mercifully the commanding officer and the adjutant had decided that our company would remain at base to guard the camp. Geoff Strong and his three junior officers appeared on parade *pour encourager les autres*.

The battalion quartermaster worked overtime to issue over two hundred shovels, large, and some emergency lighting for the operation. The whole party assembled on the parade ground and I particularly recall the sight of 2nd Lt Mole standing disconsolately wearing a huge greatcoat, with a large shovel strapped to his back and about a foot of snow piled on top of his head. Davy Crockett meets the Abominable Snowman.

We only had a few tracked vehicles, so they worked in relays taking one platoon at a time to the scene of the action. Each one was crammed with soldiers. It was as though an already overcrowded Underground train suddenly had to accommodate an extra fifty passengers in tin hats with shovels strapped to their backs.

Those of us fortunate enough to be left behind to guard the camp kept a stiff upper lip and offered lots of advice to those going to the frontline. It was with a heavy heart that Geoff Strong and I trudged back through the snow to the bar in the officers' mess.

Apparently, it was about 3 a.m. before our gallant diggers fought their way through the snow drifts to reach the outskirts of Six Mile Bottom. They then entered a polar area where the snow in some places was ten feet deep. As fast as they dug a passage to the train, another mountainous snowfall would close them down again. It wasn't until late the following afternoon that the first diggers got through.

When they finally reached the stricken train they found, to their extreme irritation, that a helicopter from Stansted had airlifted the passengers to safety some seven hours previously. Only the driver, who had refused to abandon ship, remained to be rescued. He had insisted on staying with his train until the tracks had been cleared and he could drive it to safety.

The only compensation was that, by the time the train had been freed, the Pathé Newsreel crew had driven up in a little Ford car and were able to film the triumphant scene. The Battle of Six Mile Bottom never made a general release, but it did cause some light relief to the good citizens of Bury St Edmunds and surrounding areas.

But the next time we were on the news, it was nationwide and the new TV news service carried the story right at the front of the nightly bulletin.

The snow thawed, the spring came and still the Surreys were on stand-by. By the time the Mole was putting on his cricket box and Sgt Puttman was pulling on his superfluous wicket-keeping gloves, many of us national service types were nearing the end of our service. I myself was down to seven weeks, three days, eight hours and an extremely early breakfast when I was surprised to be summoned yet again to the adjutant's office. Captain Derek Bishop told me that Colonel Clive had decided to send me on an air portability course. Apparently the Surreys had been allocated two slots on a course at a RAF station at Old Sarum near Salisbury and I was to accompany Captain D. A. N. Aldridge. I was to report at once to 'Dan' Aldridge.

I was quite mystified what air portability could possibly be, but I certainly wasn't going to show my ignorance to the adjutant, so I went immediately to find Captain Dan Aldridge. Dan was another, like Scan, who was known by his initials. He was no relation to Barry Aldridge who lost the battalion's pistols in a troopship bar. Dan had only joined the battalion at Bury St Edmunds, so I did not know him at all well. He was a portly figure whose father had also served in the East Surreys, as had his grandfather. His Dad was now a publican and Dan looked much better suited to that family business than to his family's other traditional career of professional soldiering. Certainly he looked a little out of place in the East Surreys, where the prevailing culture was athletic. There was just a hint of Billy Bunter about Dan but I was soon to learn that he was a total gent as well as a third generation East Surrey.

We had a quick discussion about logistics. Dan had a little old Morris car and he very sportingly offered to give me a lift. Apparently, it would require only the smallest of diversions to fit in lunch at his Dad's pub. So we seemed to have most things fairly well under control, except that it soon became clear that Dan had even less of a clue than I had as to exactly what air portability was.

'Balloons and that sort of thing, I expect,' said Dan, with a slight note of apprehension entering his voice.

I must confess that we looked an unlikely couple to be heading off on a ballooning course. I could only guess that somehow ballast might enter the equation and the RAF might have asked for one big one and one small one. But then again, why would two contrasting officers of the East Surrey Regiment need to learn how to fly a balloon? If we were being trained for some daring secret mission, it would have to take place within the next seven weeks, three days and eight hours, or Dan would be without his co-pilot.

It turned out that air portability had very little to do with balloons. Instead we learned the skills of loading troops, their supplies and their weapons into transport planes. If the East Surreys were suddenly to be flown to an emergency, we would all race to the nearest airfield but we would not get very far unless some of us knew how to load an armoured personnel carrier into a Hastings Transport plane. At Old Sarum we had an intensive course. The instructors were a mixture of RAF and Army and they taught us all the little tricks of the trade for loading aeroplanes. What's more, we actually had all sorts of planes and all sorts of equipment with which to play about. We could see at first hand what happens if a piece of heavy equipment breaks loose after take off, or if we distribute the weight wrongly inside the cargo bay. OOPS!

It was a brilliant and fascinating course and Dan and I headed back across the width of England to rejoin our friends in Bury St Edmunds. I couldn't help contrasting my rather stately journey with Dan in his little old Morris with the wild race across Germany with Scan in the Sunbeam Talbot. In addition, I pondered the contrasting character of my two different companions. Both were known by their initials, but that was about the only thing that Scan and Dan could possibly have in common. Dan was round and worldly, while Scan was wiry like a coiled spring. Dan was the perfect staff officer, while Scan was fired only by action and adventure. And yet these two professional soldiers both served in the same regiment. I could only reflect that the East Surrey Regiment must be a broad church.

Dan and I arrived back at Bury and two days later King Feisal of Iraq was shot dead in Baghdad. The twenty-three-year-old pro-Western King was murdered along with his powerful uncle, Crown Prince Abdul Illah. The Prime Minister, General Nuri el-Said, was kicked to death on the streets by the Baghdad mob. Our old friend Colonel Nasser had been the inspiration behind this coup in Iraq, carried out, as in Egypt, by a group of young army officers. The next day seventeen hundred marines of the US Sixth Fleet waded ashore at Beirut, where they were greeted by Lebanese girls in bikinis who handed out ice creams. Krushchev prepared to send his troops to help the plotters and Colonel Nasser. The world was poised on a knife-edge as East and West squared up over the Middle East.

At three in the morning the phone beside my bed rang; I was awakened by the familiar voice of Col Clive.

'We're off. Get your air portability hat on, Tony. I want the first battalion in Cyprus by lunchtime.' The phone went dead.

To tell the truth, the colonel was slightly pushing the deadline. His orders were to get the battalion to a staging point in Cyprus. We had to take with us every serviceable piece of equipment from frying pans to trucks and we had to be armed and prepared to fly into action in an unspecified war zone in the Middle East within forty-eight hours. This was the very operation that Dan and I had been trained for and I had hardly tumbled out of bed before the phone rang again. I recognised Dan's slightly world-weary voice immediately. Dan was a very laid back kind of guy and I was quite surprised when he started gabbling a bit on the phone. I told him to keep cool and then remembered I was talking to a full captain.

'Sorry, sir,' I said, when I had gathered my senses, and Dan then continued his instructions in a completely different and totally controlled voice. As I heard what we had to do, I immediately panicked and started to gabble myself.

'Steady, boy,' said Dan. 'Meet me in my office in thirty seconds.' And then, completely out of character, he almost barked down the phone,

'Now move!'

I was in Dan's office three minutes later. Dan was dressed and in full battledress. I was wearing a pair of sneakers, a pair of pyjamas and a sweater. In the excitement of the moment, I had grabbed my pistol. When I ran into Dan's office I put the pistol on his desk.

'What the hell did you bring that for?' he asked. I think he was concerned that I was so excited I might use it on him.

But Dan was already at work. He had road maps stretched across his desk and I saw a detailed map of Stansted airfield. Quite calmly he started passing across lists and details. He already had a whole plan of embarkation in his mind and he intended to have the first truckload of soldiers from 'A' Coy heading out of the camp gates inside half an hour. As he spoke, a bugle blew reveille and it occurred to me that the soldiers who Dan intended to dispatch in fighting order within half an hour were at that moment just waking up. The bugle call was followed almost immediately by the howl of the emergency siren. We had heard it many times before in practice and it was what the whole camp was expecting again this time. Within seconds, however, they would discover that this time it was for real.

As Dan and I talked in quick, urgent whispers, the office door burst open. Colonel Clive's huge head came round the door. He was looking smarter than he usually looked on the parade ground. He smiled a huge smile to show how much he relished the situation. His moustaches bristled and he waved his little swagger stick at Dan.

'Morning Dan,' he grinned. 'All set?'

Dan and I leaped to attention.

'Hope you two paid attention in class!' said Clive and disappeared.

As I stood there, beside Dan's desk in my sneakers and my pyjamas, I felt a ripple of excitement run through my whole body. This was it! Perhaps I did look just a little bit like Richard Todd after all.

Dan did all the tricky stuff. He set himself up at Stansted and oversaw the whole operation. My job was to drive back and forth between Stansted and Bury and try to organise the transport of the troops in roughly the sequence that Dan gave me. I had then to escort the speeding trucks to the airfield and brief the officers on loading details for their men and all their equipment. This was the nearest I would ever come to an actual military event and it went like clockwork.

There was, however, one small cloud on the horizon. I

now saw the reason that I had been sent on the air portability course as well as Dan. I was not going to Cyprus. Neither was the Mole going, nor David Ford, nor any other national serviceman with less than two months to serve. After all this drama, we would all be left behind. While Dan would climb aboard the last plane and fly off to war, we would form the rear party, go back to Blenheim Camp and help to clear up the complete shambles that was left behind.

However, at the time, I barely considered that this might be the end of a chapter. The thought that the colonel and the whole battalion might fly off in a flurry of excitement and that I might never see many of them again, never really occurred to me. I was just furiously occupied trying to follow Dan's orders and trying to get the East Surreys airborne.

There was only one slight hitch and Dan and I convinced each other that this was the fault of some bowler-hatted gent at the War Office.

On the final day of the great airlift, I escorted the regimental band to Stansted and gave instructions to Bandmaster Snowden how to load the big drum and all the instruments on the plane. He did remonstrate mildly that, in his opinion, the band would be reverting to its role of an infantry platoon and should leave the precious instruments behind. Certainly, it was true that the bandsmen were all fully trained fighting men and it seemed more likely that they would travel in that capacity, but I checked with Dan on my little radio and he confirmed he had no instructions on the matter. So he decided that the band should be prepared to play either role according to circumstances.

In fact it turned out that the band was not supposed to be going to Cyprus in any capacity. They had a prior engagement to perform at the Royal Tournament and, in the opinion of the gents in bowler hats, this took precedence over a little war. Unfortunately, though, these orders never reached the first battalion. The whole band was loaded and the plane was half way down the runway when the orders came through. A furious exchange between Dan and the Control Tower aborted the take off. The big plane just managed to skid to a halt at the very furthermost point of the runway. The plane turned and made its way slowly back to the hangar. As he came alongside Dan, the pilot wound down the side window and yelled across the runway.

'Make your bleedin' mind up, Porky.'

Dan looked up at him with total disdain.

'April Fool!' he yelled back and busied himself with his notes on his clipboard.

It was 17 July 1958.

20

A FAREWELL TO ARMS

As it turned out the East Surreys only spent a short time in Cyprus. The Mid-East crisis deteriorated into a twenty-year stand-off. Sabre-rattling around the oilfields became a major preoccupation for both East and West, with each side squaring up to the other and developing its own client states. The world's two nuclear heavyweights eyeballed each other and flexed their muscles. Neither side threw the first punch. The speedy transfer of Colonel Clive and his battalion was one tiny ripple of the muscles by our side and contributed to the uneasy peace in that area.

Unfortunately, having arrived in Cyprus for quite other reasons, the Surreys got dragged in to the Brits' own nasty war that was already underway there. Archbishop Makarios and General Grivas were pursuing a terrorist campaign and a war of attrition by which the Greek community on that island sought to drive out the British occupying forces and unite the island with Greece. It was not the sort of action which creates many heroes or easy victories. The terrorists won on points. And the Surreys, having flown out in forty-eight hours, stayed for nearly four months.

They then moved to Benghazi by landing ship to look after the elderly King Idris. Then, eventually, they returned to the UK to be merged into the Queen's Royal Surrey Regiment. We were entering already the era of the great contraction of the British Army and the decline in the prospects of advancement for many of the outstanding men who served. At the end of 1960 the last batch of national servicemen joined up. Just over five million conscripts had served in the British Armed Forces since national service had been introduced in 1939.

For us, too, it was all coming to the end. With most of our friends in Cyprus, our service wound to a close in an atmosphere of anticlimax. The Mole, David Ford and I were now the rear party back at the deserted camp. We still had to mount guard every night, but somehow our hearts were no longer in soldiering. We sat around an empty mess, played snooker and served out our last days. Tim Ross was also left behind, because he was in the last stages of being invalided out of his chosen career. Unfailingly cheerful, he commuted back and forth between the depot and Bury, bringing us news from the front and his usual retinue of lovelies.

Tim and I were involved in one last piece of action.

Because there was only a small party at Bury, the burden of duty officer, or duty sergeant, was not spread very widely. There was a great deal of idle equipment lying around the camp and it was still necessary to mount guard every night. Whoever was on duty had to forego sleep for the night. There were not many officers to take turns and there were even fewer sergeants. The regimental band made up by far the major part of the rear party, but they only sported three sergeants. One of them was called Sgt Edwards and he and I seemed to find ourselves on guard duty almost every other night. This could seriously interfere with one's normal life. For one thing, a duty officer or a duty sergeant was not permitted to hang around the bar for three or four hours. In fact they were not supposed to have a drink at all.

On one occasion, when I found myself drawn with Sgt Edwards yet again, we inspected the guard at midnight and I withdrew to my little room, where I attempted to keep my eyelids propped open through the night by reading a newspaper.

'Cyprus. Thirty-one Dead in Week of Violence' . . . 'Herb Elliott Breaks World Record for Mile'.

Suddenly there was an almighty crash. It sounded as though the camp was under a full-scale attack, or else a terrorist bomb had landed on the parade ground. I sprang from my chair. Was it possible that I was to see action in the last hours of my service? Could the Bury St Edmunds National Front have infiltrated the camp when I was on duty? Could that elusive MC come my way in the dying minutes of extra time?

I grabbed my pistol and shot out onto the parade ground. The cookhouse had been a very substantial brick-built building. It had been large enough to accommodate the whole battalion in a single sitting. But it wasn't there any more. Instead there was a heap of smoking rubble. Whatever had hit it, had exploded with terrifying force. With scant regard for my own safety, which I hoped would be noted on my citation, I ran towards the ruin.

What, in fact, had hit the cookhouse was the duty sergeant. Or, to be more precise, it was a runaway ten-ton truck driven by Sgt Edwards. Because the truck had an armoured front and because it had generated tremendous speed after two full circuits of the parade ground, it had progressed right through and into the middle of what used to be the cookhouse. As a demolition job it was clinical.

The truck still had its engine revving, but it was driven hard up against a mountain of bricks. Sgt Edwards was still sitting wide-eyed at the controls. I clambered over the remains of the cookhouse and pulled open the driver's door of the great truck. The sergeant keeled slowly over and dropped in a drunken sprawl at my feet.

''Ullo Shhir. Shhtirling Mosh,' he said before passing out.

Rather than achieving heroics in a dashing military exploit, my last action in HM Forces was to be a prime witness in a court martial. And that is how Tim Ross came to be involved. Any soldier or NCO who is charged by a court martial has the right to choose any officer he wishes to defend him. At the same time the Army can use prosecutors who are legal eagles and the equivalent of barristers in uniform. The balance is tipped against the defendant. But, in this particular case, the defendant's brief was not one that would have been too eagerly sought by any barrister, or by anyone else for that matter.

On the parade ground there had been a line-up of different vehicles that had been classified as BLR – beyond local repair. When the battalion had flown off in a hurry, these vehicles had been left on the parade ground awaiting the arrival of some mechanics from REME. Meanwhile, Sgt Edwards had shown some disappointment at being required to be duty sergeant yet again, particularly on this evening, since he had been instrumental in inviting a few sergeants from the Suffolk Regiment, whose camp was just down the road, to join his poker school and share a little refreshment. In the event, he had been persuaded that one drink would do no harm even if he was on duty and probably wouldn't be detected anyway. It was true. I probably would not have noticed if Sgt Edwards had taken one drink and, in the circumstances, I don't think I would have objected even if I had noticed. The problem was that Sgt Edwards had had closer to one hundred drinks.

Thus fortified, he had gone out onto the parade ground with a view to performing his duties. Somehow he had noticed that the ignition light of one of the largest trucks was glowing in the dark and he had conscientiously climbed aboard to investigate. At this stage, some confusion seemed to arise between himself and Stirling Moss and in a matter of a few very exciting seconds the cookhouse and Sgt Edwards' military career had come crashing down.

Poor Tim Ross was chosen as the Learned Counsel for the Defence. It was not a promising brief, but an officer who is asked to defend at a court martial is not permitted to decline. So Tim had to break away from the lovelies and practise his courtroom manner.

Of course, I was not allowed to discuss the situation with him, but I could not help pondering what line of defence Perry Mason would pursue. It seemed to me that his options were slightly limited.

'He only just nudged the cookhouse, your Honour', didn't look too promising.

Mistaken identity would be a tough one to prove since Sgt Edwards was still sitting at the wheel until such time as he slumped to his side and practically fell on top of me.

I couldn't see much future in claiming navigational error either, since the truck had obviously been travelling at a speed that made navigation largely irrelevant.

By the time the court martial was convened, I had actually experienced the pleasure of an early breakfast and I was a fully paid-up civilian. But the Army had attached a special condition to my demobilisation that demanded that I attend the court martial as a witness. So, even as a veteran, I pulled my uniform on one more time and did my duty.

The court martial was convened at Wellington Barracks in Chelsea and I was given a free lunch with the Coldstream Guards. I sat next to the duty officer and watched him eat his lunch with his hat on, which apparently is one of the strange traditions of this elite crowd. Then I was escorted across the parade ground to the small hall that was used for courts martial.

Tim Ross was the first person I recognised. He was very correct and formal, lacking only a wig. The next person I recognised was Sgt Edwards. Even though nearly three weeks had elapsed since the incident, it looked to me as though he had only just sobered up. He looked at me with a shrug as though to say,

'Don't be too hard on me.'

I was quickly into the witness box and Tim leapt into action.

'How old are you, Mr Thorne?'

I was taken aback. Tim knew very well how old I was. He had provided most of the good-lookers at my last birthday party.

'Twenty,' I replied.

'Sir!' said the elderly colonel who was presiding in the court and judging the case. 'You must address Counsel as sir.'

'Sorry, twenty, sir,' I said to Tim, trying to keep a straight face and wondering where this line of questioning was leading.

'And, Mr Thorne, would you tell the Court whether you have had much experience of drink,' said Tim.

This was definitely a low blow, since Tim had had quite frequent first-hand experience of my drinking to rather severe excess. An excess, I would have liked to record, in which My Learned Friend asking the questions had also participated.

'I, well er . . .'

'Answer the question!' snapped Counsel.

Suddenly I saw the direction of Tim's questioning. His line of argument was to suggest that I was such a young and innocent officer that I probably would not have enough experience around a bar to recognise whether Sgt Edwards was inebriated when he toppled out of the driver's cab, missing me by a quarter of an inch. The trouble with this argument seemed to me that, in the unlikely event that the court believed it, he might be doing his client a disservice. If Sgt Edwards was sober when he had demolished the cookhouse, then he was guilty of more than a breach of the Highway Code.

But, in fact Tim had done his homework and he knew that the charge of being drunk whilst on guard duty would be seen as a more serious offence than demolishing a cookhouse. In addition he coupled this argument with a plea for leniency based on the sergeant's previously unblemished record and he dragged sympathy from the Court at the thought of the sergeant's brilliant career prospects being destroyed by this one isolated, minor (did he say MINOR!) traffic incident.

Sgt Edwards was not dismissed from the service, nor was he 'Busted' all the way back to the rank of a private. He was stripped of one stripe only, down to a corporal and he was given a fine that would not have paid the cost of buying a new saucepan, let alone building a new cookhouse.

I could see right then and there that Tim Ross would not have any difficulty making his way in civilian life after he was invalided out of the Army. And that indeed turned out to be the case. Tim made his career not in the law, but in finance and he was able to put his knowledge and experience of figures to good use.

My two years' service to Her Majesty had begun with distinction at a medical examination and ended with a flourish at a court martial. The two years in-between had flown. The fact that some of the highlights and a few of the lowlights sit squarely in my memory over forty years later is vivid testimony to the value of the exercise.

It was a shared experience in which the greatest pleasure had been the company of those with whom it was shared.

In the scramble to dispatch the first battalion of the East Surrey Regiment into action, there had been no time for goodbyes. It did not even occur to me then that I might never see again so many of the people with whom I had been so fortunate to share my national service. Particularly, I would not meet again many of the regular soldiers who had earned my greatest respect.

I never saw Scan or Dan again. Sgt Puttman and Topper Brown went off for ever. Colonel Clive returned from Cyprus to be told he would not command the combined battalion of the Queen's and the East Surreys. Instead Colonel Clive retired from the Army in a blaze of affection from all who had served under him. He returned to Ireland and went to work for Guinness.

While the Mole, David Ford and I moved just down the road from Bury St Edmunds to Cambridge, some of the regulars made quite frequent appearances there. Rodgy and Ridger enlivened the campus with their infectious humour. Tim Ross, by now a civilian, provided the glamour and Dick Bing provided a steadying influence.

We organised two consecutive expeditions to the South of France, where we took our little bivouac tents and struck camp on behalf of the late-lamented East Surrey Regiment. On the second trip the Mole failed to parade owing to an unscheduled appointment with the examination board, so Webby was elected an Hon East Surrey for the duration of the holiday.

Rodgy stayed in the Army to reach the rank of captain and then found another love. She came from New Zealand and she took Rodgy back with her.

Colonel A.F. Ridger became the longest serving officer from the original East Surrey Regiment. He spent most of his distinguished career in Military Intelligence and has the same quick humour today that was his trademark over forty years ago. Dick Bing also stayed in the Army, but transferred into the Pay Corps where he established the accountancy qualifications to retire and become a successful school bursar.

For the rest of us, the temporary soldiers, we stayed life-long friends. Throughout all of my subsequent life I have enjoyed the Freemasonry that exists between those of us that were fortunate enough to serve as national servicemen.